GARDENERS' WORLD
PRACTICAL GARDENING HANDBOOK

GARDENERS' WORLD
PRACTICAL GARDENING HANDBOOK

INNOVATIVE IDEAS, EXPERT SKILLS, TRADITIONAL TECHNIQUES

TOBY BUCKLAND

PHOTOGRAPHY BY JASON INGRAM

Gardeners' World

This book is published to accompany the television series entitled *Gardeners' World*.

Executive Producer: Gill Tierney
Series Producer: Rosemary Edwards

10 9 8 7 6 5 4 3 2 1

Published in 2010 by BBC Books, an imprint of Ebury Publishing.
A Random House Group Company

Text by Toby Buckland
Photography by Jason Ingram

Jason Ingram is an award-winning garden photographer whose work appears
in countless books and magazines. He has worked on the TV programme providing
stills for *Gardeners' World Magazine* and publicity for 6 years.

The Random House Group Limited Reg. No. 954009

Addresses for companies within the Random House Group can be found at
www.randomhouse.co.uk

A CIP catalogue record for this book is available from the British Library.

ISBN 978 1 84607854 5

Mixed Sources
Product group from well-managed
forests and other controlled sources
www.fsc.org Cert no. SGS-COC-005091
© 1996 Forest Stewardship Council
FSC

The Random House Group Limited supports the Forest Stewardship Council (FSC), the
leading international forest certification organisation. All our titles that are printed on
Greenpeace approved FSC certified paper carry the FSC logo. Our paper procurement
policy can be found at www.rbooks.co.uk/environment

Commissioning editor: Lorna Russell
Project editor: Caroline McArthur
Copy-editor: Lara Maiklem
Designer: Smith & Gilmour
Photographer: Jason Ingram
Production: Antony Heller

Colour origination by Butler Tanner & Dennis
Printed and bound in the UK by Butler Tanner & Dennis

To buy books by your favourite authors and register for offers, visit www.rbooks.co.uk

CONTENTS

INTRODUCTION

'Ask not what you can do for your garden, but what it can do for you.'

I believe we are all born gardeners. It is in our DNA to want to grow and gather. We all have an 'inner gardener' that, when nurtured, yields great returns not only for your garden, but for your well being too. Gardening is not just one skill, but myriad small ones. Like riding a bike, once all the small skills come together and mastered, gardening rewards with higher self-esteem and confidence.

The other benefits are more obvious, such as healthy harvests to feed your family and an outdoor space for relaxation and play. Gardening widens your community, providing you with an amazing new natural world to explore that is full of tiny miracles which you have the gift to help happen every day of the year, just outside your back door.

There are many gardening books that advise you how to have a better garden, but this isn't one of them. This book is about how to enjoy gardening for its own sake; it's more about the means than the end. Personally, I don't want an 'end' to my gardening – a complete garden – because then how would I spend my time? Of course, your garden will benefit from your attention and efforts, but at the end of the day it is there to please and nurture you, not the other way around.

For some, the garden is just another list of jobs. But seeing your garden as a place that gives to you, rather than takes from you takes the pressure off. You don't have to have a perfect lawn or weed-free paving to be a good gardener. Your

successes might not be so obvious, and you might find just one aspect you really love, such as sowing plants from seed or nurturing orchids.

We all crave escape, whether it is from the office, the housework or just the daily grind. Your garden shouldn't be part of this problem, so make it part of the solution instead.

TAP INTO YOUR INNER GARDENER

So there you are, the season is ahead of you and the earth is ready to dig, you are ready to start your own, personal garden tradition. There are many different sorts of gardening traditions, from sowing potential prize-winning onions under lamps for Boxing Day, to plonking down in a deckchair to enjoy the first day of summer. All of them are perfectly valid celebrations of a particular time and place. I'm hoping this book will empower you to find your own gardening tradition, and a fast-track to the satisfaction this brings is to tap into your inner grower-gatherer.

Think of the big picture. You and your garden are connected to every corner of the planet. The vast majority of the plants we grow in our gardens today come from all over the world – maples come from North America, Himalayan poppies from the riverbanks of Nepal, and even vitamin-rich tomatoes come from the jungles of Peru. This connects us to other countries, as well as our own natural history, and the living heritage of the earth as a whole.

Like most gardeners, I have always been thrilled at the thought of plant hunting. But you don't have to go to Outer Mongolia to satisfy your desire for discovery. I've made dyes from woad, sweetener from Melianthus major flowers (it was nowhere near as sweet as sugar!), and string from the leaves of my New Zealand flax. These things add yet another layer of interest to your gardening, as well as a pleasant Sunday afternoon.

But the truth is, I'm less of a hunter and more of a gatherer. My gardening doesn't stop when I'm away from the garden. I think about it all the time and I have become a magpie for anything that might come in handy – bits of old timber washed up on the beach, plants rich with cuttings in a friend's garden, a nearby demolition with potential for freebies. Although garden centres are a brilliant first port of call for your garden essentials, they are not the only place to find plants and materials for your plot; any more than you would expect to get all your clothes from the same shop. Reclaim centres are bursting at the seams with pieces of old timber and readymade old benches that will give you the satisfaction of finding something different and will be a bargain too.

Even better are the unexpected opportunities that come your way – a tree surgeon with a truck-full of woodchips. He might not want them, but the paths on your allotment do. The parks' department's annual dogwood pruning has yielded trailer-loads of these brilliantly coloured stems (ideal for weaving garden supports) for my garden, and all for the price of a few pasties. It's instinctive to want to gather from your own garden too. Vegetables and fruit are a big part of this, but they are not the only harvest. The act of producing compost, reaping a chocolate-brown, sweet-smelling crop from the carefully collected peelings from your kitchen, is a surprisingly satisfying harvest.

Your garden is also a place to experience wilderness. It is your natural frontier to adventure, free for you to experiment with, a natural canvas on which you can be as be creative and productive as you like. Contrary to what many think, you don't need a lot of kit to start gardening, but always buy quality, as any experienced gardener will tell you. Secateurs, a fork and a spade are essential and I was always taught that all a gardener needed was a knife and piece of string to put things right. But as I've become more of a garden magpie, I've found that a trailer, a roof rack, some rope and bungees have come also in handy for those gatherer moments, along with, and I never thought I'd say this, a camera phone, to record those amazing-moment plants you sometimes chance upon and decide you just have to have.

You don't need to pay through the nose for things to go in your garden either. You can grow plants from seed, make your own features and draw much of what you need from your wider surroundings. It pays dividends to be brave and strike up a conversation with fellow allotmenteers and gardeners. Even if you have never spoken to them before, you have something deep in common. Making connections isn't simply about being thrifty and saving the planet either, it just feels right. While phoning around the council for green compost or chasing after horse owners for manure (which I've done and I'd recommend to anyone who can keep up a decent jog!) I have had the pleasure of meeting so many interesting and generous people. People I wouldn't know if I didn't garden. And these may well be the most valuable and life-enhancing connections of all.

GETTING

PART ONE

TO

KNOW

YOUR

GARDEN

STAKING A CLAIM

Taking on a new garden, or a new area within an established garden, is an exciting adventure. It takes some detective work to see what the soil is like and to work out what will grow and where. The fun really starts when you get stuck in and begin to pull the garden together.

From small acorns, great trees grow – it's funny how one small change can have the domino effect of leading to more. So don't be afraid to just get started, even if it's random or you start in the least obvious place; it's far worse to be paralyzed by the enormity of the task ahead of you. So start slowly nibbling away at the project and you will be amazed at how quickly an alien garden can start to look as if it belongs to you.

STARTING A NEW GARDEN

Once you have found a patch of garden to transform, start spying on your neighbours. A look over next-door's fence or around the neighbourhood will give you a good idea of the kind of plants you will be able to grow. Take pictures of the plants you like and get them identified and ordered at your local nursery or garden centre. Starting a new garden is a process to be relished, and also one that should be approached according to the situation.

OLD AND NEGLECTED GARDENS

Begin by hacking back the grass to see what comes to light – often it is old gems such as long-lived peonies and hidden gooseberry bushes. Once the grass is cut, it won't get in your way when you are pruning trees and collecting rubbish. Keep the grass out of the compost though, as it will be full of weeds. Take it to your local council green-waste collection point or stack and cover it loosely with plastic, and burn it when it dries out.

Take care when you are pruning not to chop out more than is necessary. I've known gardeners to rip out established trees and shrubs, only to replant similar replacements. Think before you cut back and rip out, and think about what your new views will look like. An over-pruned garden is rarely a private one!

CHANGE OF USE GARDENS

This often happens when children arrive or leave home. Crown lifting (see page 19) is a good way of making more lawn space for kids to play around on. And when the kids have grown up and left home, lawn lifting (see page 25) will restore the size of your borders.

MOVING HOUSE

Approach a new garden with care. If you take on major landscaping projects in winter you could dig up and kill dormant plants. Try to start work in a small area and wait to see what floral 'buried treasure' appears in the rest of the garden. You can move plants when the leaves come up, either to new flowerbeds or into a temporary nursery bed (a border where they can be left to look after themselves) until you can identify what they are. If you bring plants with you from your old garden it may be necessary to move them out of season, in which case move them straight into a nursery bed until you have time to replant them into their final position.

RIGHT: I once lost a wedding ring throwing apples in a compost bin, but at least it was in a good cause, as getting rid of rotting windfalls stops the spread of brown rot to next year's crop.

SEASONAL JOBS

When taming a wilderness, or simply controlling growth, it is often not possible to do all the work at once. Some jobs are best tackled seasonally…

■ **Spring**. Prepare the soil for planting in early spring. Trim back the remains of all herbaceous plants and grasses that are not actively growing. Rake over the soil to remove unwanted stems and 'tickle' the earth with a fork to remove footprints and any compacted areas. Spread mulch over the soil to create a neat finish ready for planting, or to feed existing plants. In late spring cut back tender plants that have been damaged by winter cold, leaving just the fresh new shoots to develop through the summer.

■ **Summer.** Hoeing is a brilliant way to get rid of annual weeds quickly – do it on a hot dry day, and once hoed, the heat of the sunshine will finish the weeds off. Give vegetable crops at least two thorough weedings as they fill out their rows and establish. In a new garden, create plenty of space around plants to give you room to weed around them. Textbooks might tell you that planting close smothers weeds, but this is only true in established gardens where weed seedlings struggle to outgrow their long-established neighbours. Prune branches that are blocking paths while the trees are in leaf, and in late summer cut back any gloomy shrubs

that may be clogging the borders. Trim overly long and neglected grass – ideally mow only half the height of the grass at one time, reducing the cutting height of the blades over a few weeks to create a lawn. Even if the grass looks bare to start with, it should green up before autumn and winter.

■ **Autumn.** This is the time for major pruning work and digging up perennial weeds, such as bindweed and ground elder. If you can, dig them out with their roots, but if you can't, at least your newly created borders will look spick and span for the winter and will be ready for covering with weed-killing mulch. Rake up, collect and compost fallen leaves. Mow around apple trees and pick up all windfall apples, otherwise they can sit on the soil and spread diseases, such as brownrot, back onto next year's developing crop.

■ **Winter.** Lift areas of lawn and dig new borders, adding lots of compost or manure to improve the soil. Trim up and shape lawns, especially around young trees, allowing for at least 60cm (2ft) of soil around the base of each tree so that the grass doesn't compete with the tree for water and nutrients. Cut back all but the best looking herbaceous plants and compost those you get rid of.

RELOCATING PLANTS

There is an old gardener's adage that you should wait for a year or two before tackling a new garden to see what comes up. I've never found this restrained approach very appealing and would far rather jump in with both feet, even in just a small area of the garden, and regret digging up hidden treasures later. I figure why wait when you can always replant flowers and bulbs that have been accidentally forked from the soil.

Whether you are moving house and want to take your favourite plants with you, have inherited a plant that is in the wrong place, or have simply made a mistake and planted something you now want to move, digging up and replanting is a skill worth mastering. It empowers you to shuffle your plants and rescue congested ones from smothering neighbours. The ideal time to do this is between autumn and early spring, before rapid growth gets underway. First, decide where your rescued plant is to go, then prepare the soil with compost and dig out a hole. This might seem counter-intuitive, but having the planting hole ready reduces the risk of the plant's roots drying out, and so increases the likelihood of the plant making a go of it in its new home.

If the foliage of surrounding plants is in the way pin them back with bamboo canes (use garden forks pushed into the soil to hold back heavy branches), then cut around the roots of the plant with a spade. Dig in a circle following the 'dripline', or outer edge, of the foliage if the plant has leaves or, if it is dormant, dig 15cm (6in) away from the crown. With evergreen shrubs and herbaceous plants you need to dig up the plants with as much soil as you can lift. Once you have pushed your spade into the soil in a circle all the way around the plant, push the spade beneath the plant and lever it from the soil. If the soil is too heavy to move, gently loosen some of it with a hand fork. Carry the plant to its new planting hole, replant it and water it in well.

RIGHT: Moving a kniphofia to a new home. When you move a plant, keep as much soil around the roots as your back can take and water well to settle it in to its new home.

TRANSPLANTING OUT OF SEASON

While the best time to dig up and move a plant is when it is dormant, this is not always possible. Here are some tips to increase your chances of a successful out-of-season move.

■ **Water well beforehand.** Leave the plants for a few hours to let the moisture soak down to the roots. If the plant is growing on a slope, rake the soil into a circular 'dam', to prevent the water flowing away.

■ **Choose the right weather.** Wait for a cool, breeze-free, overcast day to reduce the chance of the roots drying out, or work in the cool of the evening.

■ **Prune back the stems.** When a plant is dug up a proportion of its roots will be damaged or lost, making it impossible for the remaining roots to feed and keep all the leaves hydrated. How much you prune depends on how successful the move is. A large lilac, for example, will inevitably lose a lot of its fleshy roots as they fall away with the soil. To reduce the trauma if all the soil falls away, re-balance the top growth with the remainder of root by cutting the woody shoots back to as little as 30cm (12in) from the ground after replanting. That said, the more soil that moves with the roots, the less you need to prune.

■ **Move to a large pot.** Digging and potting on is a good idea even if you are not moving house and just want to move your plants around, as multipurpose compost is easy to keep moist and the pot can be kept in a shady cool spot to reduce stress. Replant in a border when the roots start to appear through the drainage holes in the base of the container – a sure sign that the plant has filled its pot.

■ **Water well after the move.** Keep the soil around newly moved plants moist by watering every other day. Give surrounding foliage a good soak too, to increase humidity around the plant. Water the plant in the very early morning or late evening otherwise the sun will scorch its leaves.

■ **Provide plenty of shade.** Use umbrellas, horticultural fleece, garden furniture or whatever is to hand to keep plants that are relocated during the growing season shaded. The hotter the weather, the more important this is – at least a week of total sun block is needed to see them well on their way to settling in to their new home.

PRUNING

Whether you are taming an established garden, or venturing into virgin territory and making a new one, pruning is always a worry… will your plants turn up their toes following surgery, and will cuts quickly made be regretted for years to come? The good news is that you would have to make a pretty catastrophic blunder for either to apply. Plants don't malinger after a haircut – if anything a brush with the secateurs will have them growing with extra vigour. Another worry is the uncertainty of whether you are 'doing it right'. Remember, no two gardeners prune in the same way, and like so many other aspects of gardening, it is as much about the heart as it is the head – if you think a pruned plant looks good, and it's healthy, well, that is all that matters!

tip

Before pruning, check behind the tree or shrub to see if its offending foliage is doing anything useful, such as blocking a neighbour's window from looking directly into your house or garden. If it turns out to be more of a help than you realized, you might do better tying the branches back to your boundaries rather than removing them altogether.

PRUNING TREES AND LARGE SHRUBS

There are two rules to keep in mind for pruning trees and large shrubs:

1. KEEP IT NATURAL

This is the arty bit… The name of the game is to make sure that what is left, after you have made your cuts, has a pleasing and natural shape. This requires more thought than merely lopping off branches. If, for example, a branch is crowding a walkway and it is pruned back to the edge of the path, you will be left with an ugly stub that will re-sprout into a tuft of growth that looks like a cheerleader's pompom, and which will be blocking the path again in no time. It is far better to prune offending branches back to the joint of another branch, or even right back to the main trunk or ground to thin out the unwanted growth. Although this might seem rather drastic, the finished effect is more graceful as the lines of the framework of branches are kept, the pruning cuts barely show and, most importantly, re-growth looks natural.

WHY BOTHER PRUNING?

Good reasons to prune:
- To let more light into your garden.
- Low branches block paths and clog borders.
- To prevent overcrowding.
- When plants have become too tall or too wide.
- There are not enough flowers low down, where you can enjoy them.
- To make leggy plants bushier.
- To enhance plants with interesting foliage.

Bad reasons to prune:
- Because you feel you should.
- To maintain spaces between plants.
- For neatness, at the expense of the plant's natural graceful shape.
- Because you get trigger-happy with the secateurs!
- Because you always do it at this time of year, whether it's the right time for the plant or not.

WHEN TO PRUNE

The time for major pruning is from midsummer (June) through to late winter. With a few exceptions (see page 21) you can cut in the spring too, but some plants bleed sap profusely at this time and you may also disturb nesting birds. Most books recommend pruning after the leaves have fallen in the autumn, but if you are trying to get more light into a garden or lift the crowns of trees so you don't get tangled up in them while you are mowing, it is better to prune in late summer while the trees are in leaf. With their summer foliage in place you can get a clearer idea of how much to prune and, because the leaves also weigh the branches down, a better idea of how much you need to cut off.

This approach also works well for unclogging crowded borders and for allowing more sunlight into shady gardens. Start with the lower branches, cutting them right back to 'lift' the crown of the tree or shrub. This will create a clear trunk and space for planting other things around its base. When pruning wide plants, aim to echo cuts on either side of the plant to prevent it looking lopsided.

tip

Prune out the larger limbs first then balance out the smaller twigs and branches to create a natural shape.

2. KEEP IT HEALTHY

This is the science bit… When it comes to the process of pruning there is a right and wrong way to do it. The right way is to cut back branches in easily managed sections from the tip to the trunk. This measured approach isn't simply about preventing hefty branches from falling on your head (although it does this too), it also reduces the risk of part-sawn branches snapping under their own weight and tearing strips of bark from the side of the tree. Torn bark is the equivalent to cuts and grazes on our skin; it creates an entry point for infections to enter the plant.

LEFT: Wait until spring to prune back the frosted stems of tender plants, like this *melianthus*, as the tops help to protect the dormant buds at the base through the winter.

For years there was a debate amongst gardeners about which was the best point on a branch to prune back to – more specifically, which areas re-grew a protective skin of bark fastest. Traditionally, branches were trimmed right back to the trunk of the tree or shrub, or to a stub that protruded from the trunk, but research has showed that the best place is in fact an area called the 'collar'. If you look at where branches join one another, or where they join the trunk, there is a raised ring of bunched up bark that protrudes about 2cm (1in) up the branch. It is easy to spot on some trees, such as apple trees, but is less obvious on others, such as eucalyptus. Regardless of this, every tree or large shrub has branch collars and this is where branches should be pruned.

When cuts are made in woody plants they don't have the ability to scab over like we do. Instead they 'compartmentalize' damaged sections to prevent the loss of sap and diseases from entering through the wound. Branch collars are a natural portcullis and because the bunched-up bark in the collar contains a higher proportion of growth cells, it means the bark is able to re-grow faster to permanently seal the wound.

PRUNING SMALLER SHRUBS AND ROSES

When you are pruning small shrubs and thin branches gradually cutting back to branch collars is not necessary, instead you should consider the plant's buds. If a bud sits on one side of a stem, then that is the direction the branch that will grow from it will point. Avoid pruning back to a bud that is pointing towards a fence, for example, or back through the centre of the plant. Always prune, if possible, to create an open-centred, graceful shape. Pruning to just above a bud keeps plants healthy as, like pruning to a branch collar, it prevents twiggy growth from dying back and potentially destroying the bud below.

PLANTS WITH SPECIFIC PRUNING REQUIREMENTS

- **Grape vines.** Only prune into old, bark-coloured wood in late autumn and early winter, otherwise the stems bleed sap profusely. Thinner 'green' growth can be pruned right through the summer.

- **Birch.** Bleeds a lot of sap so only prune if absolutely necessary from late summer to Christmas.

- **Walnuts.** Sap rises early, so prune in late summer, never winter, to prevent excessive bleeding.

- **Plums, cherries and laburnum.** Prune only on dry days during the summer. These trees are prone to a debilitating fungal disease called silver leaf that attacks and can kill the trees. Dry days are good as less of the air-borne fungal spores are around.

- **Clematis.** The popular spring-flowering species, including *C. montana*, can be left to grow large, or if space is limited trim back immediately after flowering. Late-summer flowering species, such as *C. viticella* and *C. texensis*, should be pruned back hard to 15–30cm (6–12in) in late winter or early spring. The hybrids that have large star-like flowers in the summer should be pruned to simply create an attractive shape over their support, so just cut out any old, weak or damaged shoots. If you don't do this, over time all the flowers will be concentrated at the top of the plant.

- **Wisteria.** These are so vigorous that they need pruning twice a year. In midwinter, when they are leafless, cut back all the side shoots to two or three buds from their base. In the summer, trim back the vast quantities of leafy, whippy growth to around five buds from the main branches that you have selected for training.

- **Spring-flowering shrubs.** Plants such as forsythia and ornamental currants should be pruned immediately after flowering, or you will lose next year's flowers.

- **Hedges.** Most hedges should be cut from mid to late summer, after nesting birds have flown, but before the autumn to give the hedge enough time to bounce back and look good through winter without growing so much that they look untidy again. Beech, hornbeam and holly will all recover from hard pruning if they have become overgrown. Of the conifers, only yew takes well to hard pruning, not the fast-growing leylands.

WEEDS

The worst time for weeds is spring, when every plant in the garden is making a mad dash for summer. Most weeds, such as chickweed and groundsel, are annuals that spring from seed dropped by previous incumbents. Hand weeding or hoeing, which is especially effective in the heat of summer, will deal with these. Once your garden is established and your perennial plants are coming up every year, they will help keep the weeds down by shading and out-competing them.

One of the most annoying places for weeds to grow, and the place where they are hardest to get rid of, is in paths and patios. The best way to deal with them, and to avoid chemical sprays, is to design them out in the first place. When you are making a new gravelled area or pathway, always lay down a weed-suppressing membrane onto the soil first. This will prevent most weeds from growing up through the gravel, but remove

tip

Don't put every weed in the compost bin. Unless the compost is extremely hot they won't be killed off and the worst offenders will be back. Exclude weed seeds and fleshy rooted weeds, such as bindweed, horsetail, ground elder and creeping thistle.

FACTS ABOUT WEEDS

- Always try to pull out or kill a weed before it flowers. Dock seed can live for an amazing 80 years – so much for the saying 'one year's weeds, seven year's seed'!

- Don't be beguiled if the weed is pretty. Such seductresses include rosebay willow-herb that creeps by root and prolific seed dispersal, and pink oxalis, which is almost impossible to get rid of once established due to the tubers it leaves below ground. Others might be pretty for a while, but will die off mid-season, leaving a dead, brown patch where you least want it.

- Dandelions re-grow if you don't get out the whole root, so use a hand fork or daisy grubber to dig deep.

any persistent weeds before you lay the membrane as some weeds can make their way through anything. Re-grouting patios that have become filled with soil in the gaps is well worth doing as it will prevent weeds from taking hold. If paths are already weedy, spraying will get rid of them temporarily, but they will keep coming back, so time spent weeding properly will be time well spent.

If parts of the garden are becoming too difficult to keep weed free, laying a lawn over the area is the least time-consuming way to solve the problem. Very few weeds, except lawn weeds such as daisies and dandelions, can cope with being constantly mown. Green manures such as phacelia, rye grass and clover are plants sown specifically to hold/gather nutrients in their leaves. As temporary residents they are another good treatment for weedy borders. By sowing and digging them back into the soil they will add nourishment and afford the opportunity to dig out weed roots at the same time.

On allotments, where you don't have time to be constantly weeding, instant mulches, such as paper and straw, will stop the weeds growing. Lay down newspaper around your plants at least two or three sheets thick and weigh it down with compost or stones.

I'm a keen believer in self-sowing plants, but I don't let them make a home everywhere. If they are jeopardising the health of another plant or threatening to outgrow smaller, establishing plants, or those that come up in late summer, pull them out along with the other weeds.

MAKING A NEW BORDER

Just as important as knowing how to lay a new lawn is knowing how to dig one up, as new borders usually have to be stolen from the lawn. Like everything in life, lifting turf is easy when you know how. The trick is to slice off the turf without taking great chunks of soil with it, otherwise you lose your precious topsoil and the job of making a new border is made even harder. Your best friend when lifting turf is a sharp spade, preferably made of stainless steel so that the soil will easily slide off it. Remember to bend those knees too, as it will save your back if you have a large area to lift.

Before you start, work out the shape of your border. If it is along the line of a fence it doesn't have to run parallel with it, unless you are looking for a regimented formal look. Curves, provided they are not too sharp, add character and opportunities for surprises. For example, if you have space include a curve that reaches out into the centre of the lawn and plant it with a large shrub to hide what is behind it. This will help to make a small garden appear larger and more interesting.

THE BEST SPADE FOR LIFTING TURF

1 Flat blade

2 Angled handle

3 Place this part against your knee

4 Angle of the blade under the turf

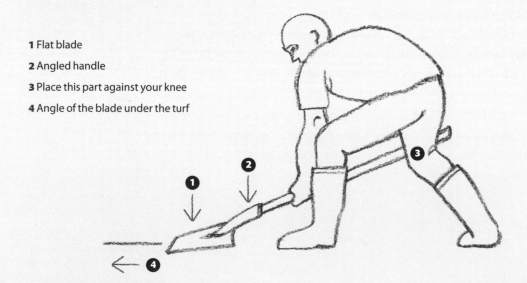

LIFTING TURF

ABOVE: With a sharp spade and a little care you can lift turf that's as flat and even as a deep-pan pizza, making it easy to relay elsewhere.

Using the sharp corner of the spade, cut parallel lines at 30cm (12in) intervals across the area of turf you want to lift, then repeat in the other direction so you are left with lots of squares that are ready to lift.

Starting at a clear edge, position the spade at an angle under the turf and push it under the grass using short 'chops', keeping the blade as flat as possible. It might be easier to place your knee against the handle of the spade to help push it into the soil beneath the grass. Then lift the square of turf and place it soil side upwards on a piece of tarpaulin or path so that the soil doesn't fall on the lawn or into the grass. Repeat until the entire area of grass is lifted.

Stack the lifted turf in a pile by the compost heap, but don't add it to your compost as it will make the mix heavy and hard to handle. Cover the stack with plastic and leave it to rot down into crumbly topsoil for raised beds and spreading through borders. Once you have lifted all the turf, work backwards to fork through the soil to relieve compaction. Add leaf mould, compost or organic matter to improve the soil ready for planting.

SETTING OUT PLANTS IN A BORDER

Brand new borders are a great opportunity to think like a garden designer and create a style. But whether you go for the prairie look or a tropical border, the key to success is to choose a good mix of shapes, textures and include around one-fifth evergreen plants. Plant the evergreens at the ends of the border or in triangles across it to hold the space together during the winter months. Perennials and grasses with interesting winter shapes will also add content to the bed. For more on choosing plants for your border, see p49.

No matter how bare the border looks don't be tempted to plant too close. It is better to use a mulch, such as composted bark or chippings, to bring the whole thing together than to overcrowd your plants to fill up the space. Mulching will also help to conserve moisture in the soil, provided you water really well first if it is high summer, and will also help to keep down the weeds.

If cats are a problem, you might want to think about some sort of deterrent, for example pieces of cut holly to discourage them using freshly dug soil as cat litter. In autumn and spring, once your plants are in the ground, add clusters of bulbs for an extra layer of colour and entertainment through the year.

RIGHT: Sow Helichrysum in spring for hula-skirt flowers, in mango and passionfruit shades, through summer and autumn.

BELOW: This dwarf dahlia 'Terracotta' is covered in flowers throughout the summer. It's a total delight in pots and window boxes.

SLUGS AND SNAILS

Forget greenfly, weevils and the dreaded blight, in my book slugs and snails are at the top of the gardener's most wanted (or should I say least wanted?) list. They wreak havoc anywhere – from attacking shoots beneath the soil in herbaceous flower borders before they even emerge in the spring, to nibbling the flowers of climbers high on the side of the house – I've even had them on houseplants! So when staking your claim to a new allotment, border or even a window box, controlling the mollusc population is a priority.

Slugs and snails, more than any other pest, are the limiting factor to what will grow in a garden – by a simple process of elimination (the elimination of your plants) they will dictate what survives... if you let them. Whenever I take on a new border or garden I start a war-like campaign to control slug and snail numbers. Not wishing to sound too much like Captain Mainwaring, the key to success is an understanding of the enemy and of the methods at your disposal to reduce their numbers. And I say 'reduce' because total victory is impossible. This is no bad thing, as it is far better to have a resident slug and snail population that is kept in check by natural predators, such as ground-beetles, frogs, toads and birds, than to have a sterile, wildlife-free garden. So while the war will never be won, if you choose your ground carefully the battles certainly can.

KNOW YOUR ENEMY!

There are more than 30 species of slugs and snails in the UK. Some have more delinquent tendencies, while others end up taking the rap for things they didn't do.

SLUGS

■ **Evidence.** Holes through the centre of leaves made by their rasping mouths scraping through the leaf surface.

■ **Worst offenders.** Keeled slug (*Milax*) – up to 10cm (4in) long and black, grey or brown in colour; it eats roots below ground and shoots above. Field slug (*Deroceras*) – 3–4cm ($1\frac{1}{4}$–$1\frac{1}{2}$in) long, grey or fawn-brown in colour; small, but deadly, it is the most damaging of all slugs and eats anything and everything that is tender and juicy, even when temperatures are cold. Black slug (*Arion*) – large, jet black and slimy, this is the archetypal slug with an orange skirt that does damage to your seedlings and young plants in spring.

■ **Lairs, dens and hide-outs.** Long grass and weeds, and leaf litter and plant debris on the soil. They love anywhere damp and dark during the day.

■ **Innocent by-standers.** The leopard slug is conspicuous because of its spots, yet they feed on dead wood and fungi and seldom do much damage to plants. Some slugs are predatory and will work for you, using their slime to melt and eat smaller slugs. They also have a taste for seedlings, though, so it is best to get rid of them if you see them.

SNAILS

■ **Evidence.** Scallop-shaped notches around the edge of leaves. Snails have biting mouthparts and prefer to gnaw the edges of leaves. They will also work on the holes created by slugs in the centre of leaves.

■ **Worst offenders.** Common garden snail (*Helix aspera*) – with a grey-brown tortoiseshell shell, it is the worst offender and has the ability to lay up to 100 eggs at a time; they can also live for anything from 10 to 15 years. Strawberry snail – up to 1cm ($\frac{1}{2}$in) wide and grey, red or pink in colour, it is less destructive, but can do lots of damage in the crown of plants.

■ **Lairs, dens and hide-outs.** Snails live amongst the stems of dense foliage and in holes and cracks in paving and walls. They hibernate in groups right through winter, huddling into dry places such as rocks, containers and in places that are sheltered from the rain. In dry weather they can survive for months without water by sealing themselves up and going into a kind of suspended animation.

■ **Innocent by-standers.** None, every snail is a bad snail, although banded snails do less damage than the common garden snail.

GETTING RID OF SLUGS AND SNAILS

Don't rely on a single method of attack – a combination is far more effective and is more likely to reduce numbers quickly.

■ **Keep your garden neat and tidy.** Clearing borders of fallen leaves, weeds and decaying stems is the best way to reduce the number of slugs and snails, which seek out the cover of leaf-litter during the day so that predators don't spot them. Where possible, clear dense grassy edges near borders. Pack out gaps in low stone walls with mortar or soil to fill in hiding places. Ivy is another popular hide-out. If necessary, reduce this fertile breeding ground by scraping the clinging stems away from walls with a spade.

■ **Encourage natural predators.** Frogs, birds, toads and hedgehogs are all allies in the war on slugs and snails. Feed birds to entice them into your garden and create a 'frog pond'. It doesn't have to be huge, a 60 x 60cm (2 x 2ft) tank filled with water by the compost heap has worked wonders for bringing frogs into my garden. If you can 'seed' it with frogspawn from a neighbour's garden, all the better.

■ **Create killing zones.** Regularly fork over the soil in borders and vegetable beds to expose snail and slug eggs, and burrowing slugs, to desiccating sunshine and hungry birds. Create a path around borders, ideally with stone or concrete paving, although compacted earth is fine. Slugs and snails won't like crossing it, but if they do, the relatively low surface area means they are more likely to encounter any slug pellets you scatter there.

■ **Slug pellets.** I only use organic pellets, which work like salt and desiccate the skins of slugs and snails. I prefer them to traditional pellets, which are laced with metaldehyde poison, as they are child and pet safe and won't harm natural predators. Scatter them along paths to protect borders, around vulnerable plants and into and around the base of climbers such as ivy, where snails tend to hide. Re-scatter after rain.

■ **Nematodes.** These are microscopic worms that have been infected with a slug-killing bacteria. They come in sachets mixed with clay dust that you dissolve in water and are so small you cannot see them even with a magnifying glass. They are expensive, but fantastic as the worms and bacteria are natural predators of slugs. By watering them amongst your plants you are delivering a concentrated dose of nematodes that will naturally decrease slug numbers.

■ **Restrain yourself.** Don't plant out dahlias, lupins, hostas and delphiniums and expect them to outgrow the attentions of slugs and snails amongst weedy soil – all you will be doing is feeding the enemy. Weed, watch and be wary!

■ **Slug traps.** Make your own organic traps that kill slugs in the tastiest possible way by drowning them in a bath of beer. My favourite design is a margarine tub with a hole cut halfway up one side. Pour 1cm ($^1/_2$ in) of beer in the bottom of the tub and replace the lid. While slugs will sniff out the sugary beer and slither in to their beery demise, ground beetles (natural slug predators) won't be able to fall in. Use them at the base of climbing plants and runner beans – I find slugs often stop off for a drink before making the ascent to the tasty foliage above.

■ **Pest patrols.** Regularly check the bases of pots as slugs tend to lay-up near the drainage holes. Patrolling the garden at night with a torch and a bucket will generally yield a good catch, especially if it has been raining. Also keep a look out for eggs while you are digging. If you find clusters of round white pearls in the soil, destroy them. And remember to watch the weather; molluscs need moist conditions to travel about, so increase your patrols and scatter more pellets during wet weather.

■ **Disposal.** If crushing molluscs underfoot, between bricks, or snipping them in half with scissors and putting them on the bird table is too much for you, then throw them over the fence. But be warned, they have a natural homing instinct and will travel back to your garden.

CREATING A GARDEN

Gardeners are often told they should have an overall plan in place before building and planting starts, but how many people really do? In truth, starting a new garden needn't be a desk job. Unless I'm designing professionally for someone else, I only put pen to paper to quantify materials. In my own garden, I get an idea for part of it and start on the ground. Small successes inform the next idea, and so on, until before you know it the garden is coming together. The planned design approach is really all about having a garden that's finished, but if you want to get the most from it that shouldn't be your aim. If you want a high-end garden then by all means hire a professional to design and build it for you, but if your garden is your hobby take pleasure from doing what you can yourself. It's more inspiring to mock up ideas outside than to sweat over a piece of graph paper. Successful gardeners sniff the air, have a good poke around in the soil, watch the way the sun rises and sets, then they get out there and seize the day. Just looking at what you've got – a plant setting its own seed for the first time or a rose briar scrambling towards a tree – brings unasked-for opportunity. Combine that with how you and your family want to use the place and you won't go far wrong.

HARD LANDSCAPING

Don't be put off taking on small hard landscaping projects – they're no more difficult than indoor DIY. If you can put up a shelf indoors, you can probably fix your own fencing or build a simple brick path for your greenhouse. Homemade features have bags of rustic charm, save you a fortune and give you far more satisfaction that anything you can buy. So have a go!

PATHS AND PATIOS

Just like the lawn, your paths and paving help shape your garden. When you are planning a garden, always think of their shape, as opposed to the outlines of borders, because they are paler in colour and stand out more.

Paths need smooth, attractive curves, and if they are straight they need to be perfect otherwise they look shoddy. Straight lines are easier to achieve, as most paving materials come in rectilinear units,

Reclaimed bricks and stones are ideal for creating rustic stepping stones, paths and edging.

tip

To lay paving in a perfectly straight line, use two pegs hammered into the ground with a taut line strung between them. If you use a spirit level to make sure it is perfectly horizontal you can also use the string as a guide for the finished height of your paving.

tip

When setting out levels, make sure paving slopes away from your house for drainage. Where it abuts a lawn, make sure it is flush with the soil level so you can mow right up and over it without catching the mower blades.

but you can make more organic shapes by using random (crazy) paving, or by spacing paving and filling the spaces in with gravel.

A common mistake is to make patios too small. Look at how much space your family needs to sit around the kitchen table, and don't be afraid to design on the ground using marker paint. Go to garden centres and builders' merchants to get ideas for materials, and bring back samples to see how it will look with your plants and house brickwork.

HOW TO LAY PAVING

It is essential to prepare the ground before you start by replacing the top few inches of soft topsoil with compacted aggregate to give you a firm base. For large areas hire a plate vibrator to get the aggregate really solid, in smaller areas you can tamp it down with the end of a mattock or pick axe.

The easiest way to lay paving is by using the five-spot mortar method. To do this you apply a dab of concrete at each corner of the paving slab and one in the middle. This allows you to glue it in place and get it perfectly level. Lay the slab down on the mortar and tap it down gently with a rubber mallet so that the mortar fills the gaps beneath the slab. Use a spirit level to make sure the slab is at the right angle and work backwards to cover the area you want to pave, leaving 1–2cm (½–1in) gaps between the slabs. Leave to dry for 24 hours then trowel more mortar (a just-moist 4:1 cement/sand mix) into the gaps and smooth with the end of the trowel. Leave to dry for another 24 hours before using.

BUILDING BASICS

■ **Cement.** This is the glue that binds sand and stone together to make concrete and mortar. It comes in a bag and looks like dust – always wear gloves when handling it, as it is an irritant. There is a range of different types of cement, some have additives to make it set more quickly or be smoother for a professional bricklayer finish, but for garden projects all you need is Ordinary Portland cement (OPC). Water initiates the chemical setting process and turns it into a workable paste. The colour varies between brands, so always use the same type for colour continuity, and store it somewhere dry otherwise it sets hard in the bag.

■ **Builders' sand.** Often called '50:50', you can buy it by the bag (convenient, but expensive) or for large projects have it delivered in one-ton bags.

■ **Sharp sand.** Washed, like builders' sand, but more angular so it locks together better. It is good as a bed for pavers or bricks.

■ **Aggregate.** A mixture of small stones and sand and the main ingredient of concrete. Buy it in small sacks or one-ton bags.

■ **Post fix concrete (Postcrete).** A quick hardening concrete, ideal for small jobs such as anchoring fence posts, bird tables and washing lines.

■ **Dyes, limes and additives.** There are a range of additives that can be mixed in with the cement or mortar while it is being made – some make it harden more quickly, dyes colour the mortar (I use hydrated lime for a chalky white finish) and plasticizers that make getting that right buttery texture more simple (a squirt of washing-up liquid works just as well).

■ **Concrete.** This is a mixture of one part cement and ten parts aggregate. Once water is added it turns into a workable paste and sets as hard as stone over a period of about 24 hours. Use for the footings of low walls and sheds and for bedding in fence posts.

■ **Mortar.** A one-part cement to five-parts sand mix that is the glue used to bed paving stones to the ground and stick bricks and concrete blocks together.

■ **How to make concrete and mortar.** When measuring out proportions either use a small bucket or do it by the shovel-load, and hire a mixer or use a wheelbarrow to mix it in. Put the largest ingredient in first, followed by the cement. Use a shovel to turn the dry ingredients and mix it all together, walking around the barrow as you go to bring the ingredients in from the edges. When the mix is an even grey colour, slowly start to add water to the centre. For mortar add more water, turning the contents with the shovel until it is as buttery and sticky as an uncooked sponge cake – it's perfect when a small amount sticks to the underside of an upturned trowel.

LAY A RUSTIC BRICK PATH

A brick path brings bags of rustic charm to a garden and is ideal for running down the middle of your greenhouse and between vegetable and flower beds. It is also a great way of using up those spare bricks that live behind the shed. If you need to buy bricks, old reclaimed ones look cottage-like and have proven their weather-durability; if you are buying new bricks choose solid clay or engineering bricks. Builders' merchants are helpful when sourcing the right quality bricks for laying on the ground, as some cheaper bricks tend to be shattered by frost.

No mortar is used for this project, the only ingredients you need are sharp sand and bricks. Expect to use around 50kg (110lb) of sharp sand and approximately 32 bricks per square metre. The technique is the same for paths from four bricks wide to entire patios.

First, dig out the area you want to pave to 2.5cm (1in) deeper than the depth of your bricks. Level it with a rake and firm down the soil with your feet. The key to success is a solid edge to stop the sand washing away from under the bricks. This could be an existing house wall; you can make an edge with 12cm x 2.5cm (5in x 1in) treated timber planks set on edge into the ground, with the top at the same level as the top of your bricks. Hold the plank firm by knocking timber pegs into the ground at 1m (40in) intervals and screwing the timber planks to them.

Put down a weed-suppressing fabric on the soil and cover it with a 2.5cm (1in) layer of sand. Use a piece of timber to firm and flatten the sand then lay bricks on top of it in staggered rows, tapping them down so they are level with the timber plank edges and each other. Once all the bricks are laid, shovel more dry sand across the top and brush it into the gaps to lock them together.

WOODWORK PROJECTS

■ **Decking** I'm not ashamed to say I'm a big fan of decking. It's simple to lay and covers all manner of problem areas, such as ugly concrete, dips and hard-to-plant stony ground. Information on how to build decks is everywhere, but I have some tips of my own. Never skimp on the bearers (the wood used to create the frame). I use 5cm x 15cm (2in x 6in) thick treated timber for a really solid, bounce-free feel. I also use these same chunky timbers for the surface as, unlike purpose-made decking boards, they weather and turn silvery over time. It's more economical to buy timber rough-sawn rather than planed – you can remove any rough edges and splinters once it is laid by jet washing it, which is something you should also do once a year to keep it clean and free of slippery algae.

■ **Fences** Fence manufacturers have done a good job of making us think that fencing panels should be something ornamental to look at. Personally, I think fences are something you try to hide!

When choosing ready-made panel fencing it is easy to be beguiled by twiddly trellis tops. For me, the most important attribute of a fence is its strength, which gives it longevity and will save you money in the long term. I always recommend a closeboard fence, which is made up of overlapping feather-edge boards that are fixed to a framework of horizontals called arris rails. Both sides of a closeboard fence look good, and the arris rails are useful for running wires for climbers along. It is also better for following the contours of your garden, whereas panels have to step up and down which can look ungainly. It is easier to replace old fences with closeboard as you can adjust where you put the fence posts, which means you won't be limited to using the old post foundations.

If you do choose to use panels, stick to one type otherwise your fences can start to look disjointed. Domes and arches work well in small areas, or as internal divides, but they are expensive and run the risk of looking too fussy if used in long runs.

■ **How to put in fence posts** Whether you buy fence panels, make your own featherboard and arris, or are simply repairing a falling-down fence, you will need to fix fence posts. If you are

tip

Use bamboo cane to mock up 3-D structures, such as sheds and pergolas, to give you a feel of what they will be like to live with.

Stacking stones and bricks together to make low walls is as old as civilization. At first glance, building with stone looks complicated, but all it really requires is a cook's ability to mix ingredients (sand, cement, water), to make a 'glue', and a little care to stack the stones neatly. This method is ideal for building walls up to around 50cm (20in) high, which are perfect for low walls, retaining walls, seats or path edging. If you need anything taller you should either seek help from a professional builder/waller or arm yourself with more know-how by going on a weekend stone walling course or taking an evening class.

Before starting to build, sort your stones – lay them out flat to make picking and choosing easier. Ideally the stones should be dry, as this helps the cement stick, so cover them with plastic for a few days before you plan to lay them.

Dig a hole for your foundations. For a low wall around 50cm (20in) high, I use the tried-and-tested method found in Victorian houses and simply scrape away the top 10cm (4in) of soil in a strip about 25cm (10in) wide (1). Then pour a mixture of one part cement to eight parts sharp sand (mixed in a barrow) into the bottom 5cm (2in) of the hole (2). This creates a

bed that, once set, ties the base of the wall together.

Next mix the mortar (3–6, see p.35). Like the foundation mix, this should also be mixed in a barrow. For a traditional white finish that will match the stone, add a trowel of builder's lime (3).

Trowel the mortar along the bottom of the hole, on the layer of set concrete, and set the largest stones with their flattest side facing outwards where you can see it (7). Once the bottom row is in place, select stones that will fit neatly on top and trowel mortar between the joints of the bottom row (8) – add enough mortar so that when you drop the next course of stones in place it spreads to fill out between the two stones. As you build up, use a level to check that the face is upright. Scrape spilled mortar from the face of the stones and prop up the back of the stones with lengths of wood, or if the wall is retaining, by packing sharp sand down behind them. If you are building a low retaining wall, leave small gaps between the stones on the bottom layer, at about every metre, to allow water to escape from behind the wall (9).

Before the cement fully dries, use a wire brush to clean the stones (10 and 11) and smooth the mortar to highlight their faces.

tip

Use a small bucket to measure out the sand and cement before mixing. If the proportions of your ingredients change, so will the colour of the joints when the mortar dries.

tip

If your mortar mix is too wet, mix 5:1 parts sand and cement in a bucket and gradually add it to the main mix. This will soak up some of the water, while keeping the consistency the same.

putting up a brand-new fence on level ground it is best to start with the posts at either end of the run, as they will dictate the finished level of all the posts in between.

Run a taut line along the boundary, keeping it straight, and dig a hole roughly a quarter of the length of your post – if you want a 2m (6ft) fence you will need to buy 2.5m (8ft) posts and bury them 60cm (2ft) in the ground. Get a friend to hold the post while you pack around the base with bricks to stop it wobbling and to pour in the concrete. Use temporary timber battens, knocked into the soil at an angle and screwed to the post, to stop it moving while the concrete sets. For a speedy job use quick-drying fence-post concrete. An alternative to concrete is metal fence spikes that are knocked into the ground then the posts are slotted into them, but unless you are working on virgin, stone-free ground these can be tricky to get in perfectly upright. Run a second string line between the very tops of the two end posts to give you the height of those that go in between. If you are erecting closeboard use the gravel boards that run along the base of the fence to stop the featherboards from rotting, as a measure for where to dig the next hole. If you are putting up panel fences, use a single panel to judge the distance.

SOIL TYPE AND ASPECT

Soil type and aspect determines what you can grow in a garden. A lot of hand-wringing goes on about soil type – clay, loamy, sandy, chalky – and pH, but extreme soil types are less prevalent than the vast amounts of copy written about them would have you believe, and also very apparent. Acidic soils are identifiable by locally growing rhododendrons and blue-flowered hydrangeas; chalky soils by obvious pieces of white chalk in the ground and very thin soil; and clay soils puddle after heavy rain and are sticky when wet.

No matter what hand you've been dealt, all soils, no matter how bad, can be improved by digging in organic matter (see pp.80–5) or with the help of raised beds (see p.43). Just make sure you do your digging when the soil isn't waterlogged or

PLANT UP WALL CREVICES

■ The best technique to establish
flowering plants in wall crevices is to mix
seed into a blancmange-like slurry of wct
soil with (and you're probably not going to
like this) plenty of horse manure blended
in. The blended soil and manure should
be about the size of a tennis ball, to this
add a packet of seeds, take a pinch of the
mixture and smear it into a wall crevice.
Do it in all the nooks and crannies and
water it in with a mister. If you don't fancy
using manure, you could use wet well-
rotted compost instead – it's less sticky,
but less stinky!

■ Alpine plants are ideal for this
treatment, such as the purple bellflower
(*Campanula poscharskyana)* or fleabane
(*Erigeron karvinskianus),* with its almost
year-round daisy flowers, wallflowers and
old favourites such as aubrietia and chives.
Hardy succulents such as stonecrops
(*Sedum acre* and *S. rupestre)* give an
instant effect, simply use the soil slurry
to glue the roots in place. For the shady
side of a dry wall, try planting hart's
tongue fern near the foot or top of the wall
and let it spread naturally. Hart's tongue
fern will also grow in sun, while wall-rue
(*Asplenium ruta-muraria)* and the hardy
fern *Polypodium vulgare* prefer it damp
and shady.

MAKE A TIMBER-EDGED RAISED BED

Choose chunky timbers, such as reclaimed 5cm x 2½cm (2in x 6in) roof joists. They might seem heavy to lay, but they are long lasting and it's far easier to make perfectly square beds with these than with thinner timber. They can also take a bit of bashing about when you're digging among the beds later.

The beds should be situated in the sun for vegetables and can be any length, but no more than 1.2m (4ft) wide so you can reach in to tend crops at the back without stepping on the soil. Dig over the site and the adjacent paths first, lowering the paths by about 5cm (2in) and piling the spoil onto the bed area(1). Position the timber edging where you want them to go and fix them together at the corners with long screws (2).

Using a spirit level, adjust the sides so that they sit level (3) – remove or pack out with soil as necessary. Check that the bed has right-angled sides by measuring the diagonals and hammer timber pegs (two for each side) into the soil alongside the timbers (4). Fix the sides to the pegs with wood screws. Finally, fork through the soil in the bed with a third of a barrow load of compost per metre, then add more topsoil as necessary to bring it up to within 2.5cm (1in) of the top and rake the soil flat (5).

frozen, or you will turn the cold in and potentially spoil the soil structure.

In terms of aspect, whether your site is sunny, shady or, as with most plots, a mixture of both, determines what you can grow. It is something that you can only learn by observation, taking the time to notice where the sun lingers and where the sun rarely reaches – often the same areas where the frost tends to sit. If your borders face south and west you will have the widest choice of plants. While east- and north-facing borders might see less sun, early flowers such as daffodils will last for longer and, provided the spot is sheltered, can provide a haven for lush-leaved foliage plants.

RAISED BEDS

One way to get over poor soil in any garden is to create raised beds, particularly if you want deep soil to grow vegetables. They don't need to be raised very high; 15cm (6in) is fine, as this allows you to add a greater depth of topsoil and a few barrow loads of compost. It also has the effect of improving drainage, warming the soil in cold gardens and providing more nutrients for hungry plants such as vegetables. It is also a neat way of compartmentalizing your vegetable patch from other parts of the garden, to deter the trampling feet of pets and children.

DESIGN WITH PLANTS

In terms of design, aim for one-fifth of your garden to contain permanent structures or evergreen plants, with the rest split between flowers that really stand out and flowers or ground cover that knits everything together to hide the brown soil. Look for opportunities to train plants and to garden in unlikely places, such as the tops of walls, roofs and between paving slabs. It's creative and enjoyable, whilst giving you the chance to interact with your garden, and getting you away from the usual 'jobs' that can leave you feeling that the garden is nothing more than an endless round of mowing and weeding.

TREES

They used to say that you plant a tree for your grandchildren to enjoy, but these days there are plenty of fast-growing small trees that make a good size in just a few years. Trees are great for natural privacy and provide so much more – shelter, a perch for swings and birds, and a way of connecting your garden with the wider landscape and sky. While flowers bring your garden to life in summer, trees do sterling work either in spring with their blossom or autumn when the foliage of deciduous trees turns to gold. It might not be summer, but it's some consolation if there is a bucket-load of apples to pick, or a Japanese cherry covered in scented blossom.

HOW TO PLANT A TREE

When you are planting a container-grown tree, first place the pot in a bucket of water to soak, then dig a hole about four times the width of the pot and just a little deeper than the rootball. Fork over the base of the hole to break up the soil so the roots can grow down more easily (1) then sprinkle half a bucket of garden compost and a handful of bone meal into the hole (2). Knock the tree from the pot (3) and place it in the centre of the hole, adjusting the amount of soil underneath the rootball so that the top of the pot compost is 1cm (½in) below the surrounding soil level – too deep and it can rot the trunk; too shallow and the rootball runs the risk of continually drying out.

Hammer a stake into the ground next to the trunk on the side of the prevailing wind, so the tree doesn't get blown against the stake (4). If you are planting in an open site put the stake on the southwest side, as this is where wind blows from the majority of the time. In built-up areas wind is more likely to swirl around, so observe where it comes from the most and stake on that side of the tree. Secure the trunk to the stake with a rubber tree tie. Except for dwarf fruit trees, which remain staked for their whole life, remove the stake after two to three years.

Trees are vulnerable to drought and will need watering in dry weather up to two years after planting. Make a raised ring of soil 2.5–5cm (1–2in) high, 30cm (12in) from the trunk to stop water run-off and use a full can of water to settle it in its new home (5).

tip

Prune laburnum and Japanese cherries when they are in leaf as spores of silver leaf fungus can infect cuts, causing first the branches then, eventually, the whole tree to die.

For the best autumn colour on Japanese maples, plant in lime-free soil in the sun.

tip

For permanently waterlogged soils, plant willow and keep them coppiced, chopping down to a stump every few years. If the soil tends to sit wet in winter, good choices include Rowan (*Sorbus aucuparia*), hawthorn (*Crataegus laevigata*), snowy mespilus (*Amelanchier canadensis*) and river birch (*Betula nigra*).

Specialist nurseries often sell trees as bare-root plants, rather than in containers. This means they are grown in the soil then dug up in the autumn for sale, which doesn't do the tree any harm and makes them more economical to buy. Bare-root trees are only sold in the dormant season, whereas containerized trees can be planted at any time. When you take delivery of a bare-root tree, soak the roots in a large tub of water and don't delay planting, unless you are forced to by very wet weather or a heavy frost. Plant bare-root trees as you would trees grown in a container.

HEDGES

tip

The best time to prune or trim hedges is September, when the birds aren't nesting and the hedge has time to leaf up before winter.

Both trees and shrubs (see p.49) can be used as hedges, but if you use a tree it has to be one that will tolerate regular clipping. Though most people prefer evergreen hedges, such as yew and holly, for privacy, it's worth also remembering that some deciduous hedges retain their young leaves, such as beech and hornbeam.

GREAT GARDEN TREES

■ **Japanese cherry.** If it's blossom and autumn-tinted foliage you're after, choose a cherry. For an oriental look choose *Prunus* x *yedoensis* for its lacquer-black bark, when wet, that shows of the pom-pom pink flowers and tiered branches. *P. sargentii* is a martini-glass shape and good for growing in tight spots, close to boundaries. For that classic wide bower of white blossom, choose 'Taihaku'. There are also purple-leaved cherries, *P. cerasifera* and cherries that flower in autumn/winter, such as *P. autumnali*. Cherries don't need pruning, but if cutbacks are necessary only do it in summer to avoid silver leaf and canker. Ideal for all types of soil, cherries grow up to 6m (20ft) tall by 6m (20ft) wide.

■ **Birch.** The tree with the best white bark is the Himalayan birch (*Betula utilis* var. *jacquemontii),* and varieties bred from it. It grows into a goblet, spaced as little as 2m (6ft) apart, so it lends itself to mass planting in small places. Our native birch, *B. pendula,* has branch tips that hang down like a wizard's sleeve, creating a peaceful, natural look. Birches drop a lot of twigs in winter, but the up side is that you can tie them together to make a besom broom! Good for any soil type, even thin, grows up to 10m (33ft) tall and 6m (20ft) wide.

■ **Maple.** Not all acers grow into trees. The Japanese maples (*Acer palmatum* Dissectum) grow very slowly into living boulders, but all do best in sheltered gardens out of leaf-shredding cold winds and in deep, lime-free soils. One of the best is the coral-bark maple, *Acer* 'Senkaki'. It has three seasons of interest: bright-red young winter stems, pale-green emerging leaves in spring and rhubarb and custard tints in autumn. For the best autumn colour, choose *Acer* 'Osakazuki' – come autumn the small, delicate palmate leaves look as if they have been set on fire. Acers grow up to 6m (20ft) tall and 5m (16ft) wide.

■ **Crab apple.** Beautiful hardy trees with spring blossom and bucket-loads of ornamental fruits in late summer and autumn, good for any reasonable soil. 'John Downie' and 'Veitch's Scarlet' produce the best fruits for jams and jellies, while 'Red Sentinel' is my favourite for a more ornamental look with its small, bright-red, bauble-like fruits that hang on until after Christmas. *Malus trilobata* looks more like a small acer, thanks to its palmate leaves and neat shape, but with the added bonus of not just autumn colour but blush-green fruits. Can grow up to 10m (33ft) tall and 8m (26ft) wide.

■ **Mimosa.** Once only found in the mild south-west, warmer winters have led this winter-flowering *Acacia dealbata* to be grown more widely, in the south-east, sheltered gardens and in urban areas in full sun. Its best features are the lovely blue-grey foliage and honey-scented yellow tufted sprays. Plant in free-draining soil, such as a sunny bank, and go for my favourite and the hardiest, *Acacia longifolia.* Up to 10m (33ft) tall and 6m (20ft) wide.

■ **Mountain ash.** Also known as rowan, these are hardy, graceful trees that are tolerant of all soil types, even chalk, and are known for their berries and autumn colour. One of my favourites is *Sorbus vilmorinii*, with autumn-tinted leaves, fruits the colours of pink champagne, clusters of pendulous white flowers and lovely feathery leaves that create a gently dappled feel and, on a practical note, compost quickly in your leaf bin after they fall. For silver, felty leaves and red berries choose the whitebeam *Sorbus aria* 'Lutescens'; it is brilliant for coastal and exposed conditions. Sorbus make neater trees than crab apples as there is less dropping debris, and you won't mind the birds eating the berries. Grows between 5–10m (16–33ft) tall and 4m (13ft) wide.

tip

Site hollies, hawthorns and black locust trees (*Robinia pseudoacacia*) where the spiky debris that falls from the branches won't be a problem.

POPULAR HEDGES

HEDGING	SOIL	ASPECT	EVERGREEN	GROWTH RATE	SIZE	PLANTING DISTANCE	GOOD FOR...	PRUNING
Beech (*fagus sylvatica*)	ordinary alkaline	sun/semishade	keeps leaves through winter	medium	1.5–4m	40cm	formal and rural look	prune in September
Holly (*Ilex aquifolium*)	ordinary, heavy clay	sun/shade	Yes	medium	1–3m	45cm	Formal and wildlife	prune in September
Yew	ordinary, clay chalk	sun/shade	Yes	slow	1.5–3m	60cm	formal look	June and September for formal look
Box	ordinary, clay, chalk	sun/shade	Yes	slow	20–120cm	30cm	low hedges	after frosts, again in September
Hornbeam	ordinary, clay, chalk	sun/semi-shade	keeps leaves through winter	medium	1.5–4m	40cm	formal, or rural	September
Cherry laurel (*Prunus laurocerasus*)	ordinary, clay, chalk	sun/semi-shade/full shade	Yes	fast	2–4m	60cm	formal and informal	with secateurs in August
Western red cedar (*Thuja plicata*)	ordinary, unfussy	sun/semi-shade	Yes	fast	1.5–4m	60cm	formal	September
Rosa rugosa	ordinary, shallow, clay	sun	no, hips persist into winter	fast	1–2m	45cm	cottage, wildlife	late winter
Cotoneaster lacteus	ordinary, chalky	sun, semi-shade	Yes	fast	2–3m	45cm	flowers, berries	late winter
Hawthorn	ordinary, clay, chalk	sun, semi-shade	no, but dense and thorny	medium	1–2m	45cm	flowers, berries	August

tip

When you are trimming a hedge, cut it so the sides slope towards the top and light can reach the leaves at the base of the hedge. Use secateurs for plants with large foliage and shears and hedge-trimmers for those with small leaves.

If you only want a small hedge, use faster-growing evergreen shrubs such as *Viburnum tinus* 'Eve Price' and autumn-scented *Elaeagnus*. Conifers are often chosen because they are fast growing, but Western red cedar (*Thuja plicata*) is a far better choice than a Leyland hedge, which never stops growing and has led to many unpleasant boundary disputes. See the table above for more popular hedge plants.

HOW TO PLANT A HEDGE

The most economical way to plant a deciduous hedge is with bare-root plants in winter, while evergreens are sold in pots. Plant just as you would a shrub (see p.52), but it is essential to keep the plants evenly spaced. The best way is to dig out a trench and improve the soil for your hedge with well-rotted manure or garden compost all in one go. Peg out a string line end to end for a straight hedge and set out plants using a spacer made from a bamboo cane to keep them evenly spaced. All hedges bush out better if the top quarter of growth is pruned off after planting. The most important care for a new hedge is to water, I do this by placing a seep-hose right along its length to give roots a really good soak whenever it's hot and dry.

Put up a temporary windbreak of netting before planting a hedge in a garden that is exposed to cold easterly winds. This will protect the hedge for the first couple of years while it is establishing.

SHRUBS

Shrubs have been out of vogue in recent years, with garden designers if not your average gardener, as longer-flowering and more dynamic perennials and grasses have become more fashionable. This is less down to the shrub and more down to how shrubs get used in the border. Novice gardeners often go wrong by focusing on flowers, which may only last for a few weeks, rather than leaves, and plant so close together they end up looking like a green, shapeless mass for most of the summer. This also tends to mean they get over-pruned and lose their natural, graceful shape. But shrubs deserve better; they are very useful for creating privacy, structure and a backdrop to your borders right through the year, with seasonal highlights of flowers, scent or berries.

Evergreen shrubs give a garden year-round character and structure, and just a few go a long way. Three of the same type, positioned in a loose triangle across different borders, will tie a whole area together when all else has gone to ground. Deciduous shrubs often have a single season of interest, so take care to plant it next to something that looks interesting at a different time.

Purple-leaved shrubs have the richest colour if they are not over-fed with nitrogen. Stick to the occasional feed in summer with a high-potash fertilizer or seaweed tonics to ensure they look their best.

MAIN SHRUBS

Small (up to 60cm)	SOIL	ASPECT	GOOD FOR ...	PROBLEMS
Acer palmatum var. *dissectum*	neutral–acid	any	slow-growing specimen; lovely spring leaves; autumn colour	avoid exposed windy spots
Ceratostigma willmottianum	well-drained, ordinary	full sun	fast-growing; good for edging; blue summer and autumn flowers	prune hard if it gets straggly
Cotoneaster horizontalis	ordinary, unfussy	full sun/ semi-shade	fast-growing; good for wall-training and banks; spring flowers, autumn red berries	use mulch to suppress weeds under low branches
Lavender 'Sawyers'	well-drained, poor	full sun	fast-growing evergreen; good for hedging and attracting wildlife; aromatic with purple wands	don't cut into old wood; shear into hummocks after flowering
Pittosporum 'Tom Thumb'	ordinary	sun	evergreen; good for formal borders; purple green-tinged leaves	hardy in all but the coldest gardens
Small/Medium				
Cornus sanguinea 'Midwinter Fire'	ordinary, moist	full sun/ semi-shade	fast-growing; good for hedging and beside water; orange-red winter stems	hard prune before leaves emerge biannually
Euphorbia x *pasteuri*	ordinary	any	fast-growing evergreen; exotic-looking with a honey scent, like x *mellifera* only bigger and better	irritant sap, wear long sleeves when deadheading
Sarcococca hookeriana var. *digyna*	ordinary, fertile	shade/ semi-shade	evergreen; good filler for shade; winter scent	gently spreading, remove unwanted suckers
Medium (60cm–1.2m)				
Ceanothus 'Puget Blue'	neutral–alkaline, well-drained	full sun	fast-growing evergreen; good for poor soils, hot walls and makes good screening; blue spring flowers	short-lived – 10–12 years
Daphne bholua 'Jacqueline Postill'	ordinary	full sun	semi-evergreen; good for small front gardens; winter scent	don't prune as tends to die back
Hebe 'Midsummer Beauty'	ordinary, neutral–alkaline	full sun/ semi-shade	fast-growing evergreen; good for hedging, topiary and in coastal areas; long-flowering, nice shape	needs shelter from cold winds
Hydrangea paniculata 'Tardiva'	moist, ordinary	full sun/ semi-shade	fast-growing; good in cold areas; late-summer, white autumn flowers, make good dried flower	prune hard in spring
Magnolia stellata	ordinary, alkaline	sun, not morning sun	slow-growing specimen; spring flowers	plant in spring out of frost pockets, don't disturb roots

	SOIL	ASPECT	GOOD FOR ...	PROBLEMS
Mahonia x *media* 'Winter Sun'	ordinary	shade/ semi-shade	evergreen specimen; good for front gardens and attracting wildlife; scented yellow flowers in winter	reduce leggy stems in spring
Myrtus communis subsp. *tarentina*	ordinary, well-drained	sun	evergreen architectural specimen; good in pots; scented white summer flowers	needs protection in cold gardens
Rhododendron luteum	fertile, acid	full sun/ semi-shade	Oriental look, woodland style; scented yellow flowers in spring, autumn tints	shelter, mulch in spring
Med/Large				
Osmanthus x *burkwoodii*	ordinary, well-drained	full sun/ semi-shade	evergreen; good for back of borders and hedging; spring scent	plant in shelter to trap scent
Phormium tenax	ordinary, unfussy	full sun/ semi-shade	fast-growing evergreen; exotic	tougher than cordyline but protect in cold areas
Pyracantha 'Saphyr Rouge'	ordinary, unfussy	full sun/ semi-shade	fast-growing evergreen specimen; good for wall training and hedging; white spring flowers, red autumn berries	thorny
Large (over 1.2m)				
Buddleia davidii 'Black Knight'	ordinary	full sun	fast-growing; good for attracting wildlife; dark purple flowers	hard prune in February
Camellia x *williamsii* 'Donation'	moist, neutral–acid	semi-shade	evergreen, good for screening; pink spring flowers	avoid east-facing situations
Cornus kousa var. Chinensis	fertile, neutral–acid	full sun/ semi-shade	specimen; spring flowers and autumn tints	mulch annually with leafmould
Corylus maxima 'Purpurea'	ordinary, unfussy	full sun/ semi-shade	fast-growing; good for nuts, pea-sticks and hedging; purple foliage and good for rods	prune out a fifth of branches to the base every year for rods
Syringa 'Charles Joly'	ordinary, alkaline, poor	sun	small tree; good for cottage gardens and backdrops; purple scented flowers in spring	take out a few old stems annually

LEFT: Bold yellow swathes of Rudbeckia bring late-summer borders to life.

RIGHT: Clumps of lavender look stunning and smell great too.

tip

Variegated and golden-leaved shrubs are good for breaking up ranks of sombre green, and as they tend to scorch in full sun are best used to light up gloomy areas. Snip out any shoots that revert to green – because they have more chlorophyll they will be more vigorous and will outgrow the paler leaves.

HOW TO PLANT A SHRUB

The ideal time to plant deciduous shrubs is autumn, when the soil is warm and moist and it is easy for the plant to get established. For evergreens the best planting time is spring, when the risk of desiccating winter winds has past. Chances are, however, that you will want to plant as soon as you buy your plant – often when it is in flower – which could be any time of year. This is fine, provided soil isn't waterlogged or frozen. Keep an eye on the watering once it's in the ground and with evergreens, if your garden is exposed to cold winds, protect young foliage with fleece or netting.

Getting the site right is important too. Once a shrub has been in the ground for three years it won't like being moved and may die if it is dug up and transplanted, unlike perennials. Like trees, shrubs are long-lived so they need good soil preparation to grow at their best. Water the shrub well before planting, dig a hole at least three times the width of the pot, fork over the bottom of the hole, adding garden compost as you go, and sprinkle a handful of bone meal over the soil to help promote root growth.

With large shrubs, I hold the trunk in one hand and knock all around the rim with the palm of my hand until the pot slips away. Loosen up the roots of 'pot-bound' plants, to help them spread out into the soil, and pop the rootball into the hole. Stand back to check the best side of the shrub is facing you, backfill with soil and tread it in so there are no air pockets, ensuring it's at the same level as it was growing in the pot. Water it in until the soil puddles and keep it watered through dry spells in the plant's first year.

GRASSES AND BAMBOO

Large grasses and bamboo can be used as substitutes for shrubs and to bring life to a border. Grasses prefer well-drained soils and sunshine, while bamboo is a better choice for moist, shady spots. Large grasses die down in winter; the dry stems will remain standing, but have to be cut down to stumps in late winter to allow the fresh blades through. If you want evergreens, choose a bamboo.

Medium and small grasses look best grown in prairie style, repeated across borders, so it's a good idea to sow them yourself to keep costs down. They all germinate freely and are often up within a couple of weeks. The ones that flower early, such as tussock grass and reed canary grass, should be grown in a porch or greenhouse. Late-season grasses that like hotter weather, such as *Pennisetum* and *Miscanthus*, come up best in a propagator set to 20°C (68°F).

Collect the seed when it's fluffy and either sow immediately in the autumn or keep it in a labelled envelope for sowing in the spring. Don't prick out plants individually, as you would for flowers, instead, once seedlings sprout, separate them and pot on as clumps to bulk up more quickly. Named varieties may not come true from seed, but the progeny will still be good.

HERBACEOUS PERENNIALS

When it comes to planting flowers, the big issue is long-lasting colour. The way to achieve a colourful garden is, of course, by

USEFUL GRASSES AND BAMBOO

Maiden grass (*Miscanthus sinensis* 'Gracillimus'). An elegant, tall grass with late-summer flowers, holds its plumes long into winter. Cut back to stumps in February before new leaves appear. Grows 1.2m (4ft) high.

Feather reed grass (*Calamagrostis* x *acutiflora* 'Overdam'). Similar to the lovely upright sheaves of popular 'Karl Foerster', but smaller and with more presence in early summer, thanks to variegated leaves and pink feathery flowers. Cut down in February, grows to 1.2m (4ft) high.

Fountain grass (*Pennisetum alopecuroides* 'Hameln'). Good for front to mid-border, lovely with hot-coloured perennials thanks to its bottle-brush-style flowers and curling leaves. Grown to 1.2m (4ft).

Arundo donax. Bamboo-like, large grass, great for a jungle-effect in sunny, warm gardens and for the back of the border. Grows up to 5m (16ft).

Toe toe grass (*Cortaderia richardii*). Smaller, more compact pampas grass with a year-round presence. Tidy up and remove old leaves in winter. Grows up to 2m (6ft).

***Deschampsia cespitosa* 'Goldtau'.** See-through puffs of flowers that grow in shade right through summer. Has a year-round presence, just comb out dead leaves and remove flowerheads in winter. Grows to 1m (40in).

Bamboo (*Phyllostachys*). All the commonly available bamboo species make good garden screens in shade, as they are relatively non-invasive. For black stems choose *P. nigra*, for golden stems *P. aureosulcata* f. *spectabilis*, and for thick, tropical-looking exotic canes choose *P. vivax* f. *aureocaulis*. All grow up to 10m (33ft).

Bamboo (*Fargesia mureliae*). Stripy, thin, graceful stems that form a dense clump, this is the one for narrow alleys down the side of your house. Grows up to 4m (13ft).

Bamboo (*Fargesia rufa*). The best bamboo for cold gardens, green canes with pink young growth. Can also be grown in a pot. Grows 1–2m (3–6ft).

Bamboo (*Fargesia robusta*). Upright growth and zebra-striped culms give this medium-sized neat bamboo a tropical look. A great specimen plant and screen, grows 2–4m (6–13ft).

planting a good range of flowers that bloom at different times of the year for a 'succession', which comes and goes in the same patch of soil. One way to do this is to go visiting garden centres and nurseries in every month of the year to see and potentially buy new plants already in flower. Although many garden books tell you not to buy plants in bloom, this is one of the best ways to view the exact shades for your colour scheme provided you can resist the temptation of too many impulse buys!

The vast majority of perennials start to grow in spring, flower in summer, die down in winter and come back every spring. Of course, there are exceptions. Some perennials, coneflowers for example, tend to be very short-lived, while

tip

Repeat planting combinations all along the same border, or in different borders, to give a garden a sense of continuity.

GOOD PERENNIALS

	SIZE	ASPECT	SOIL	FLOWER	COLOUR	GOOD FOR...	AGM
Astrantia major **'Shaggy'**	small	sun/semi-shade	ordinary	summer	white-green	cottage	yes
Crocosmia **'Lucifer'**	med	sun/semi-shade	ordinary	summer	red	exotic style	yes
Dicentra formosa alba	small	sun/semi-shade	alkaline	summer	white	woodland	
Echinacea purpurea **'White Swan'**	small	sun	ordinary, moist	summer/autumn	white	prairie style, winter interest	
Epimedium perralderianum	small	semi-shade	moist	autumn		woodland	
Eryngium bourgatii	med	sun	well-drained	summer	blue	drought, winter interest	
Euphorbia griffithii **'Dixter'**	med	semi-shade	ordinary	summer	red	spring stems	yes
Geranium **Rozanne**	small	sun/semi-shade	ordinary	summer	purple	filler	yes
Geranium **'Ann Folkard'**	small	sun	ordinary	summer	magenta	golden leaves	yes
Helenium **'Moerheim Beauty'**	med	sun	ordinary	summer	mahogany	prairie style, winter interest	yes
Helleborus x hybridus	small	sun/semi-shade	heavy	spring/winter	pastels	winter	
Hemerocallis **'Stella de Oro'**	small	sun	ordinary	summer	yellow	pots	
Heuchera **'Purple Petticoats'**	small	semi-shade	ordinary	summer	white	pots/fillers, winter interest	
Hosta **'Patriot'**	small	shade	moist, ordinary	summer	white	variegated foliage	
Knautia macedonica	med	sun	ordinary	summer	burgundy	wildlife	
Kniphofia uvaria **'Nobilis'**	med	sun	ordinary	summer/autumn	red/yellow	exotic/hot border, winter interest	yes
Lychnis coronaria **'Alba'**	small	sun	well drained	summer	white	silver foliage	yes
Macleaya microcarpa **'Kelway's Coral Plume'**	large	sun	ordinary			back of border	yes
Nepeta racemosa **'Walker's Low'**	small	sun/semi-shade	ordinary	summer	blue-purple	filler/front of border	
Paeonia officinalis **'Rubra Plena'**	med	sun/semi-shade	heavy, rich	spring/summer	purple-red	cottage	yes
Papaver orientale **'Patty's Plum'**	med	semi-shade	well-drained	summer	plum	cottage	
Penstemon **'Garnet'**	small	sun/semi-shade	ordinary	summer/autumn	pink-red	cottage	
Phlomis russelliana	med	sun/semi-shade	ordinary, dry			filler, winter interest	yes
Rudbeckia var. *sullivantii* **'Goldsturm'**	med	sun	ordinary	summer	golden	cottage, winter interest	yes
Salvia nemorosa **'Ostfriesland'**	med	sun	ordinary	summer/autumn	purple	prairie, cottage	yes
Scabiosa caucasica **'Miss Willmott'**	med	sun	ordinary, alkaline	summer	white	cottage, prairie, winter interest	yes
Sedum gypsicola **'Herbstfreude'**	small	sun	ordinary, well-drained	summer	salmon	cottage, winter interest	yes
Thalictrum aquilegiifolium **'Thundercloud'**	med	semi-shade	ordinary	summer	lilac	cottage, natural	yes
Tiarella **'Iron Butterfly'**	small	shade/semi-shade	moist, ordinary	spring/summer	white	foliage filler	
Verbena bonariensis	large	sun	ordinary	summer	purple	cottage, airy	yes
Veronicastrum virginicum **'Fascination'**	tall	sun/semi-shade	ordinary	summer	blue/mauve	prairie, winter interest	

FROM LEFT: All winners for early spring colour: *Viola*; *Euphorbia myrsinites* and Red valerian (*Centranthus ruber*).

others, such as cranesbill geraniums, live for years if they are divided every three to five years to regenerate growth. A few prefer not to be disturbed at all; these tend to be plants with very fleshy roots, such as peonies and Japanese anemones. Asters really only get going in summer, so you need to give them a spot on the edge of the bed or collect them together in groups or 'drifts' to give them a fighting chance of getting the light they need to perform.

Spring bulbs and perennials that die down by midsummer, such as bleeding heart, make good bedfellows too. Then there are perennials that don't die down at all, such as elephant's ears (*Bergenia*) and *Heuchera*. These make excellent edgers for defining beds when all else has gone to ground; they also make brilliant front-garden plants to welcome you home year-round. A precious few even flower in the depths of winter, such as the beautiful hanging saucers of hellebores and elephant's ears. These benefit from having any winter-tatty leaves cut back before the flowers emerge.

Perennials come in a wide range of sizes and habits which lend themselves to different garden uses: the low-growing spreaders, such as cranesbill geraniums, *Erigeron* and catmint, are brilliant as 'fillers' over the bare soil between taller upright flowers. These fillers are also good for spilling over the front of borders and hiding bare legs of shrubs, particularly roses.

tip

Cut off dead flowers, either to the stem or to a new set of buds. Where flower stems sprout from the base of the plant, cut the whole spent stem back to the ground with secateurs (unless you are leaving it for winter interest).

Others are airy, making low, unobtrusive clumps of leaves with flowers atop wiry stems, such as *Verbena bonariensis* and angel's fishing rods.

HOW TO PLANT PERENNIALS

Assuming you've bought your plant in a container, the first thing to do is to make sure it goes into the ground moist – I always stick mine in a bucket of water to soak while I'm preparing the soil. Plant when the ground is moist and easy to dig, never when it is frozen or soaking wet. If you've got a few to plant, get a barrow of soil improver (stuff from the compost heap or leaf mould) and throw in a few trowelfuls in each planting hole to give plants a good start.

In spring, if there are young bulbs or tender shoots coming up, put an upturned hanging basket over the top of them to prevent them being trodden on. It's easier to dig the holes for most plants with a spade, but use a trowel for those grown in the smallest ½-litre pots. Dig your holes just a little deeper than the root-balls, but twice as wide, leaving the spoil next to the hole ready to fill back around the roots.

Everyone has their own way of getting the plant out of the pot, but my method of dislodging the roots from the container without damaging them is to turn the pot upside-down, hold the plant against my palm with the crown nestled between my outstretched fingers, then knock the rim of the pot against the handle of the spade until the plant slides from its container. If the plant has only recently been potted on the compost may fall easily from the roots, so get it into the ground quickly.

Plants that have been in pots for some time will have circling roots that should be gently pulled apart; not completely, but just enough to encourage them to grow out into the soil rather than continuing to grow round and round. Once it is in the hole, support the crown by holding the stems with one hand and brush soil gently over the exposed roots, firming it down with the tips of your fingers, or for large plants the flat of your foot. Always water plants after planting to settle them in and don't forget them when it's dry and hot, and especially if it's dry and windy as this quickly draws the moisture out of leaves.

tip

Don't worry too much about planting in odd numbers, anywhere between three and eight plants makes a good block if planted in loose, unregimented groups or ribbons through borders.

LOOKING AFTER YOUR PERENNIALS

Perennials are fairly self-sufficient but they do have needs. The first thing to remember is to watch that the young growth is protected from slugs and snails when it is first emerging. This is less of a problem with perennials that keep all or some of their foliage through the winter and those with tough or aromatic leaves, but it is essential for plants such as delphiniums and lupins that have very soft juvenile leaves. Vulnerable leaves appear at the time when the usually moist spring weather creates favourable conditions for slugs, but provided you can get plants up and away, they will get to a size where they won't be killed by the odd nibble.

Stake your plants with twigs or shop-bought wire hoops early in the year, so that they grow into their supports and hide them. Push the support into the ground so that the tops are roughly two-thirds of the eventual height of the plant. Not all plants require staking, although in windy gardens keep some sticks handy as an insurance policy!

With new plantings you need to water at the first sign of prolonged hot weather or drought. Don't hang back and wait for plants to wilt as this will check the plant's growth and set back flower production. The same goes for taking off the dead flowers; unless you want to grow a plant for its seedheads, or if the plant is sterile (as with many double flowers), removing the spent flower stalks will stop the plant wasting energy on setting seed and encourage it to continue producing more buds.

Of course, every perennial has its time to flower. This is normally late spring/early summer, midsummer or late summer into autumn. Those that flower in early summer often have another flush and almost a second spring if it is a warm September. Cutting back the old foliage, which tends to look a bit tatty after flowering, can encourage this. Even if you don't get flowers it still refreshes the foliage and makes a better backdrop for the maincrop of summer perennials.

Come autumn, flower stalks die back and plants start to flop and go to ground. In a wet autumn it can all become a bit of a soggy mess, so I tend to wait for a dry day in November to get in and have a blitz, cutting back all the stems bar those that still look good. They will last until after Christmas and along with the grasses, which you don't cut down until February, will make sure the beds don't look bleak and bare right through until the spring. Any with stems that are still stout are left to catch the frosts, but when they do topple, chop as low as you can to the ground leaving as short a stub as possible; it looks neat and you don't catch your hand on the stumps when weeding later.

Autumn is also the optimum time to lift and divide perennials that have spread and become bare in the centre (see p.117). Only some plants need to be divided in the spring – grasses, crocosmia, and any tender plants that flower in late summer. As soon as you notice a bald patch in the centre of a plant, during summer, push in a label as a reminder to take action when it is dormant later in the year.

ROSES

Roses are beautiful summer flowers; often deliciously perfumed and either coming all at once in clouds of blooms (once-flowering) or producing flushes right through summer (repeat-flowering). You can buy plants in two ways: container-grown, which is ideal if you want to see the colour of the flower, or bare root, which is the cheaper, traditional option. Bare-root roses are field-grown, dug from the ground when they are dormant (between November and February) and sold without any soil on the roots.

ROSE VARIETIES

It used to be the case that the old garden-centre categories of climbers, floribunda, hybrid tea and shrub roses dictated the way you used them in the garden, but the boundaries have since been blurred by breeding. Flori-shrub roses, for example, are hybrids between small floribundas and larger shrubs. They can be clipped into more formal shapes or left to grow into graceful, arching bushes. The same can be said of the modern shrub or 'New English' roses, such as 'Graham Thomas', which are real multi-taskers. Bronze 'Buff Beauty', for example, can be left to mound in a border, be trained as a climber against a fence, or spun round an obelisk – and it flowers all summer long.

Beware of the old roses, though. They may be wonderfully

tip

Some plants, such as Japanese anemone, resent disturbance, so instead of lifting the whole plant it's best to leave the plant in place and chop divisions from the edge of the clump.

scented and have the most romantic names, but many are weak growers and disease-prone. This may not be the case if you are lucky enough to have perfect rose-growing conditions – an improved clay soil and full sun. For a really large rose to grow in a tree, choose a rambler, such as the disease-resistant, cloud-white 'Rambling Rector'. Unlike climbers that have upright briars and tend to repeat-flower, ramblers have lax, thorny stems that are good for scrambling to the top of the canopy and produce just one glorious flourish of blooms in June.

HOW TO PLANT ROSES

The way to plant roses is deep. Rose varieties don't grow on their own roots, they are grafted onto the rootstock of another seed-sown rose to guarantee good vigour. The peculiar, knobbly lump at the base of the stems is the graft point, where the shoots join the roots. When planting you should bury this graft 5cm (2in) below soil level. This encourages the flowering stem to develop roots, looks less ugly and ultimately encourages stronger growth. Dig out a hole at least 45cm (18in) square and fork in some well-rotted manure. It is also worth sprinkling the roots with mychorrizae (see p.222) to aid fast establishment and encourage disease-free growth.

ROSE CARE

Roses are prone to three fungal diseases: rust, powdery mildew and blackspot. Rust shows up as orange splodges on the undersides of leaves and is promoted by damp, stagnant conditions. Powdery mildew is a white, talc-like covering on leaves and also yellow patches. It tends to occur in hot, dry conditions. Both rust and powdery mildew can be dealt with by modifying the conditions in which the rose is growing or by moving them to a more suitable place.

Blackspot, on the other hand, can cripple roses. It looks, as its name suggests, like unsightly black spots on the foliage. Many old rose varieties can't be grown without repeat-sprays of fungicide, or the use of the naturally occurring mineral, sulphur, which can be sprayed as a tonic onto the foliage. Sulphur is an element in sulphur-dioxide, one of the chemicals

PROLONG THE COLOUR

Finding plants that flower in April, May and June is easy – even for people who don't garden. Out-of-season colour, on the other hand, is another matter. Apart from going out of your way to plant for colour at those times, there are other techniques:

■ **Cut back after flowering.** This is fashionably called the 'Chelsea Chop', because certain plants are cut down after the Chelsea Flower Show when they are starting to look tired. Late-spring and early-summer flowering perennials respond well to this, including cranesbills, geraniums, lady's mantle, columbine and oriental poppies. Do the same in August with plants that have come to the end of flowering and are looking tatty, but where you can see the fresh foliage in the crown, such as herbs like oregano, mint, lemon balm and fennel.

■ **Cut back before flowering.** Cut back late-flowering plants that tend to flop in flower, such as chrysanthemums, Veronicastrum and perennial sunflowers. Trimming back in June with shears helps to keep them bushy and doesn't delay flowering. You will get smaller, but more abundant, flowers on shorter stems.

■ **Plant bulbs deep.** This is a good technique for pots or cut flowers. Plant the same bulb at a range of depths for a succession of blooms – an inch deeper and it will flower after those planted more shallowly.

■ **Remove dead flowers.** Take off dead flowers unless you want to save the seed or enjoy structural seedheads. As soon as plants go to seed they stop producing blooms so removing dead flowers will keep plants flowering for longer. This technique is particularly important for annual flowers and bedding plants, such as sweet peas.

in smoke pollution, which is one of the reasons why roses used to be so healthy in Victorian times and in central city locations.

There are other ways to reduce the effects of this disease – choose varieties such as the lovely white *R.* 'Macmillan Nurse' or rugosa roses and check out online nursery lists for roses labelled as 'blackspot-resistant'. Plant in as much sun as possible, as drier air makes infection far less likely. Make sure the plant has what it needs to grow healthily and fight off disease by mulching over the roots with a 2.5cm (1in) layer of garden compost in the spring, which will help the soil to hold on to moisture during the summer, and feed with a specific rose feed during the growing season. Spraying the leaves with liquid seaweed fertilizer will also make the foliage more lustrous and difficult for fungal spores to get a toehold. Water the plants

tip

Remove the spent flowers from repeat-flowering roses and herbaceous plants to ensure you get a fresh flush of blooms. Cut the dead flower stalk back to the nearest stem or fresh set of buds.

only in the morning if possible, and avoid wetting the leaves as black-spot spores only spread if the leaves are wet. Clear away the mulch and the fallen leaves in the autumn to remove any old spores and always remove and burn affected leaves when you see them.

BULBS

I love bulbs. They come like sweets in paper packets full of the promise of flowers to come. What you have in your hand when you hold a bulb is an embryonic plant – leaves and flowers all folded by magical origami and simply waiting for warm, moist soil to unwrap and release them.

There are hardy bulbs that survive outside all year-round and tender varieties that don't like cold. The latter are kept under cover in winter, potted up in spring and planted out for the summer, before being brought back indoors with the beginning of the frosts. There are also so-called borderline varieties that will survive if the soil is well drained and it is warm and frosts aren't prolonged. I have used the word 'bulb' as a generic term to cover bulbs, corms and rhizomes, which require similar treatment in the garden.

HARDY SPRING BULBS

If you're the kind of person who finds the winter months a misery, then spring bulbs are the answer. Plant bulbs around perennial crowns as they die down in autumn and be generous, spreading them right across borders. Daffodils can be planted as early as August and tulips can be planted as late as December, but no earlier than October. The rule of thumb when planting hardy bulbs is to plant at twice their depth and spaced twice their width apart. So, a 5cm (2in) -tall bulb should have 10cm (4in) of soil above it. There are exceptions, though; hyacinths go in one and half times their depth and tulips three times.

I prefer to reserve daffodils, narcissi, snowdrops and squills for more natural schemes, along banks and pathways in cheery crowds, or in areas of lawn that can be left to grow longer as foliage dies down and replenishes the bulb. Pot up and grow

tip

Bulbs generally do best and live longest in freely draining soils, so they are an ideal choice for sandy soils or raised parts of the garden such as banks where rain quickly drains away.

tip

For natural-looking drifts of daffodils in grass, plant types that suit wilder situations, such as the Tenby daffodil (*Narcissus obvallaris*) and Lent lily (*N. lobularis*) for early spring trumpets, followed by pheasant's eye daffodils to take the display into May. Avoid planting in blocks, instead throw the bulbs in the air and plant them where they fall.

on small bulbs such as Dutch crocus, and those with a more artificial look such as hyacinths and dwarf iris in the greenhouse to bring them into bloom a good few weeks earlier than those grown outdoors.

The earlier bulbs flower, the smaller they tend to be, so mass-plant purple *Crocus tommasinianus* in grass and dainty *Narcissus cyclamineus,* with its swept-back petals, for best effect under deciduous trees and shrubs. Snowdrops, cyclamen and the collared, yellow, buttercup-style flowers of winter aconites are difficult to establish from bulb, but both can be bought in growth and planted out where they will spread on their own into naturalistic drifts.

For February and March the choice is wider – carpets of electric blue squills and chionodoxa, trumpet daffodils, and snakeshead fritillaries for soils that don't dry out. April is the tulip's month, the single cups of Darwin, followed by the beautiful range of shapes and colours in May, from the fringed parrot tulips (wonderful in pots) to the elegant nipped-in vases of lily-flowered types. Tulips aren't long-lived, especially in heavy soils, so the answer is to lift the bulbs and store them somewhere cool and dry as soon as the leaves have died down, alternatively grow them in pots.

After flowering finishes, it's tempting to cut off dying-down

LEFT: Dahlia 'Garden Wonder' grows to lower than waist-height, so it's good for pots and late summer colour.

RIGHT: Daffodil bulbs are economical to buy in bulk to use to create sheets of colour in spring.

tip

Some bulbs are best in pots, either because they're delicate, such as dwarf iris, or too brash for borders, such as hyacinths.

YEAR-ROUND HARDY OUTDOOR BULBS

Spring flowering:
Jonquils, Tazetta for path edges/pots, Tenby daffodil (*Narcissus obvallaris*) and Lent lily (*Narcissus lobularis*) for natural drifts, hybrid daffodils (for borders), Tulips, snake's head fritillary (*Fritillaria meleagris*), Anenomes (*Anemone blanda* and *Anemone nemorosa*), English bluebells, grape hyacinths (*Muscari*), glory of the snow (*Chionodoxa*), *Scilla*, dog's tooth violet (*Erythronium*), summer snowflake (*Leucojum aestivum*), *Trillium*, crown imperial.

Summer flowering:
Cardiocrinum for shady, moist and sheltered areas, ornamental onions (*Alliums*), camassia for damp soil, Turk's cap lily (*Lilium martagon*) and *Lilium regale* are both good for cool shade), *Agapanthus* Headbourne hybrids (the hardiest African lily), Star-of-Bethlehem (*Ornithogalum umbellatum* and *Ornithogalum nutans*, foxtail lily (*Eremurus*), bearded iris.

Autumn flowering:
Hardy cyclamen (*Cyclamen hederifolium*), *Colchicum*, *Crocus speciosus*, autumn squills, Madonna lilly (*Lilium candidum*).

Winter flowering:
Snowdrops, winter aconites (*Eranthis hyemalis*), crocusi (*Crocus tommasinianus*, Dutch crocus, and *Crocus chrysanthus*), Cyclamen (*Cyclamen coum*), *Iris unguicularis*.

bulb foliage because it looks scruffy, but the leaves nourish the bulb so wait until they turn papery and pull away easily – at least six weeks after the flower dies. Allium foliage looks dead while still in flower, so close-plant filler foliage of catmint or geraniums to hide it. Spanish bluebells make all their leaves after the flowers have appeared, which can be very invasive, so deadhead spent blooms to curb their spread.

HARDY SUMMER BULBS
Summer bulbs are a brilliant way to pack in more colour, adding another layer to existing flower-schemes and impact to drifts of perennials. Try *Allium sphaerocephalon* and *Nectaroscordum* to lift sunny late-summer borders or, provided you don't crowd their crowns with the foliage of other plants, the magnificent flower spikes of foxtail lilies (*Eremurus*).

Lilies, on the other hand, are better in containers. Although I couldn't do without their wonderful summer scent I now restrict all my lilies to pots as the lily beetle – a pillar-box-red

tip

Dwarf Asiatic lilies, traditionally sold for container planting, are short on scent, so plant the more fragrant, but taller, *Lilium regale* in spring and weigh them down with pebbles and heavy loam-based compost to prevent them being blown over. Feed with a high-potash fertilizer every fortnight in the run-up to flowering for top-class blooms.

insect whose grubs devours the leaves (see p.225) – has made growing lilies in borders a risky challenge. With the plants in containers you have a 360-degree view of the plant and can kill the grubs and beetles before they do any damage. Plant them up in autumn or early spring for summer scent and colour.

Though spring bulbs are planted in autumn, many summer bulbs can be planted as late as March for flowering the same summer, including some alliums, many species of lily, foxtail lily, arum and autumn snowflake.

BORDERLINE SUMMER BULBS

If you live in the south of the country or parts of your garden are warm, well drained and frost-free, you can get away with growing borderline bulbs outdoors. Raised beds or at the base of sunny walls are optimum spots, where the soil is baked and stays dry in winter. South African bulbs such as late-summer-flowering tulbaghia, pineapple lily (*Eucomis*), galtonia and the bright pink stars of nerine do well here and, if the soil is sufficiently free-draining, they can be left in the soil, otherwise they should be transferred into pots and kept dry through the winter. Topping up the area with a 5cm (2in) mulch of grit will help to insulate them and keep them alive to see another year. The alternative is to grow these bulbs as pot plants, transferring them outdoors in the clemency of summer and keeping them on the dry side in the greenhouse during the winter. Remove

Dainty *Tulbaghia violacea* is perfect for terracotta pots placed in a sunny spot, or at the base of warm, sunny wall.

HOW TO GROW DAHLIAS FROM TUBERS

Dahlia tubers look like fat fingers that are joined at the top beneath the stump of last year's main stem. To plant tubers, bury them in 2–3 litre pots filled with multipurpose (peat-free is fine) compost, making sure last year's dead stem is pointing upwards. Water carefully and keep them in a greenhouse, or coldframe, away from the frost. Start to put them outside during the day in early May to harden off the foliage and ready them for life outside. Once the frosts have finished in late May or early June, dig a hole and plant so the knuckle where the stem joins the tuber is buried by about 5cm (2in). This will give the stems more stability. Stake the plants with pea sticks, creating a hidden supportive frame for the flowers to grow through. Remove dead flowers regularly and keep watered in dry spells. In autumn, dig up after the first frost and bring in and keep dry indoors, alternatively, if your soil doesn't sit too wet in winter, you can leave dahlias in the ground, provided you mulch the ground where they're buried with a 5cm (2in) layer of garden compost or grit to keep the cold off.

tip

Dahlias can be grown in pots in a sunny spot on the patio. Choose a dwarf dahlia, such as 'Terracotta', which is covered in small, salmon-coloured buttons from early summer until the frosts.

begonia tubers from pots and dry them off to reduce the risk of damage from vine weevil.

Gladioli, also from South Africa, aren't hardy either, but they can be planted out in March straight into borders for flowering the same summer. Bed them out in bulb baskets if you want to lift them for replanting next spring, or treat them like disposable bedding plants. I like to use gladdies as a replacement for lilies. While they don't have scent, they flower around the same time, have greater number of blooms and are available in carnival colours. Plant a few corms in groups of three every few weeks through spring for a succession of vivid flower spikes and swords of leaves from July into autumn. In the south, *Gladiolus byzantinus* and the white *Acidanthera murielae* are perennial in a warm spot and well-drained soil.

TENDER BULBS

Truly tender bulbs, like bedding plants, are summer-only visitors but with the advantage that you can keep them year after year with a bit of care. Buy or order your bulbs in the winter or early spring, pot up in a greenhouse in March and jump-start them into growth so that when they are planted out in a warm, sheltered place after frosts have finished, they are large enough to bloom. They are late-flowering and in an Indian summer you can have borders aglow with rich ruby-reds, crimsons and gold right into November. What's more, these summer visitors are a good way to fill gaps in newly establishing borders while waiting for permanent plants to mature. Because they are dug from the ground every autumn, it also allows you to get on top of weeds when the ground is empty.

Grow fleshy-rooted canna lilies, ginger lily, begonia and chocolate cosmos as for dahlias (see opposite). Plant bulbs of pineapple lily (*Eucomis*), tulbaghia, tiger flower (*Tigridia*) and *Acidanthera* in pots of multipurpose compost, spacing them 5cm (2in) apart, two-thirds down the pot.

tip

Prune hybrid 'Jackmanii' and *viticella* clematis in late winter or early spring before they start to grow down to 30cm (12in) from the ground, otherwise they become bare at the base. Alternatively, leave them to do their thing and to mound, with all the flowers at the top.

CLIMBERS

Not all climbers are the same. Some clad, some mound and sit on top of a support, while others can be grown as border plants. Climbers are handy in new gardens to add height and give more of a feeling of enclosure. They are also good in mature gardens when you've run out of space, as they grow upwards to occupy space higher up, and can also double up with a tree or woody plant as an extra layer.

CLADDERS

Some of my favourite plants are cladders, which add a layer of living colour to fences and walls. Climbing roses, hybrid clematis, the hugely spreading and self-clinging Virginia creeper and dramatic variegated ivies all do a good job. The key is to plant them at least 50cm (20in) out from the wall or fence and tilt the rootball so the stem is leaning towards where they're going to grow up.

Self-clinging passion flowers, Boston ivy, Virginia creeper, ivies and the climbing hydrangea (*Hydrangea petiolaris*) all have sticky suckers to hold them to the support. No wires or trellis are needed, but the supports must be in good condition

otherwise the suckers will get into the brickwork or literally pull a rickety fence apart.

Twining climbers, such as wisteria, climbing roses and hybrid clematis, need wires to cling to. Many people don't bother, but it is the only way to get your climber to grow where you want it, otherwise it is just as likely to follow the sun and meander off next door. A neat way to do this is to use vine eyes – screws with circular 'eyes' on the end that can be screwed into timber fences or drilled into walls with rawl plugs.

Fix vine eyes horizontally, in rows 45cm (18in) apart and spaced every 1.5m (5ft). Make them look neat by ensuring all the eyes are at the same level along the support and not higgledy piggledy. Run wires through the eyes and to get them guitar-string tight my trick is to use a pair of pliers to twist the vine eyes at the end of each run, turning the wire around the shank of the vine eye.

Other good cladders include wall shrubs such as fig trees, spring-flowering ceanothus, and berry-producing firethorn. These aren't true climbers but do a brilliant job of hiding fences.

MOUNDERS

These are climbers that tend to scramble up the support and create a great bird's nest on top, which means they are ideal for the top of porches, sheds and for covering tree stumps. Scented jasmine, rambling roses, trumpet creeper, the spring-flowering *Clematis montana*, the larger honeysuckles and the evergreen potato vine (*Trachelospermum jasminoides)* are all good for this job. Wires and vine eyes can help to support these plants, but instead run the wires vertically up pillars to help get stems to the top more quickly.

Smaller mound formers, such as sweet peas and shrub roses, are ideal in borders supported by wigwams, as are the very versatile hybrid clematis species.

tip

Help self-clinging climbers, such as ivy and Virginia creeper, to stick more quickly by trimming back the old stems by a third at planting time. This will encourage a spurt of fresh, new, self-clinging growth.

tip

Climbers have to cope with tough, dry conditions due to their proximity to drying concrete foundations that draw moisture from the soil. For climbers in south-facing positions, always add plenty of soil improver to the planting hole and keep them well watered for the first couple of years when it's hot and dry and until the roots are fully established.

Clematis roots like to be kept cool and moist, so always plant them a hand's width deeper than they are in the pot and cover the soil surface with slates or stones to shade the roots.

LEFT: *Clematis armandii* 'Apple Blossom' makes a good large cladder for sun-soaked walls and fences and flowers in late winter and early spring.

OUT-SOURCING

My garden isn't an island, it's integral to the rest of my life and that of my family, quietly enriching every day. Once you get out and into your garden you will soon see how addictive it can be. It starts innocently enough, perhaps noseying at some allotments as you pass by on the train and picking up some ideas for yours. The next thing you know you have become a veritable magpie, always on the lookout for bits and pieces to feather your nest – old timber to turn into compost containers and manure from a horse-riding friend to enrich its contents. Noting a tree surgeon at work or a demolition digger knocking down an old building becomes not just the cause of an inconvenient traffic jam, but an opportunity to get some freebies.

Connections to the garden deepen even further where the kitchen is concerned. Fresh food comes in and peelings for the compost heap go out, along with a regular supply of slug-deterring coffee-ground mulches. But being a garden magpie isn't just about saving money, although of course it does that too, it is about satisfying a need. It connects you back to something innate and instinctive – your inner hunter-gatherer – and in modern life any chance to get in touch with the universal should be seized with both hands.

WHERE TO RECYCLE AND RECLAIM

Half the art of recycling is seeing the value in what is available – what might be a pile of soggy leaves to one person is soil-enriching compost to a gardener, and best of all it's free! A pile of washed-up driftwood is not just debris, it can be a garden shelf, a seat, an unusual garden ornament or a plant wigwam. Spotting a seed head full of ripe seed and ready for the taking gives me the same feeling of abundance and harvest as seeing a full skip, a salvage yard or a blackberry bush weighed down with juicy berries. Here are some of the best places to find free, recyclable and reclaimed stuff for your garden:

Tree surgeons. Look out for tree surgeons with a shredder on the back of their trailer. They are a great source of chippings for paths, and the tree surgeons may even be able to deliver them to you for the price of a round of beers. Tree surgeons are also a good source for firewood, stick plant supports, sawn logs for rustic seats, timber edging for borders, and branches with sculptural shapes and interesting bark. If they don't have what you want they will often keep an eye out for you and deliver it to your door.

Local woodland trusts and parks departments. This is the best place to buy hazel rods – the pea-stick plant supports you see in grand National Trust gardens. Every few years many woodland and wildlife trusts cut down the branches of trees in their managed woodlands, to allow light down to the forest floor. The added benefit of buying these coppice products is that you will also be supporting your local environment.

Oh look, another bit of lovely salvage-tat from the recycle centre to stash with the rest behind my garage. You never know when it will come in useful!

GARDENS ARE FOR SHARING

■ **Don't throw anything away.** If you are a keen seed sower you will always have more seedlings than you need. Save any unusual varieties, such as heritage tomatoes, to swap with other gardeners.

■ **Buy in bulk.** Fellow gardeners and allotment holders all need the same things, so form a buying group to get discounts on fleece, feeds, etc. You will also spread the cost of postage at the same time.

■ **Share your gluts.** This doesn't even have to be like for like. I used to trade peas with my allotment neighbour and in return he mowed around my vegetable beds.

■ **Buy your local paper religiously.** Keep an eye out for good deals on soil improver, wood chips, manure and local authority-sponsored composters.

■ **Many hands make light work.** If you have a large job, such as putting up a shed or fence, throw a Shaker-style building party. You provide the tools and materials, along with some refreshments, and what would have taken you a year can be done in a day.

■ **Thatchers.** These craftspeople are one of the main users of freshly cut hazel, as it is used to make the pegs that hold the straw or reeds onto roofs. Because they need so many, thatchers often have a sideline in managing local woodland and are only too happy to sell you some supplies.

■ **Reclamation and salvage yards.** Old tin baths work well as plant containers and compost holders, water tanks are perfect as water savers, old furniture is good for potting benches, and roofing slate, bricks and reclaimed stone make characterful cottage-style paths and walls. Greenhouse frames and old windows can be made into coldframes and cloches, and iron gutters and cast-iron hoppers make great plant containers. Timber, including scaffolding planks and reclaimed wood, is good for making wooden swing seats and recycled bin stores.

■ **Your own garden.** Pick comfrey to make liquid fertilizer (see p.86). Grass clippings are good as a free alternative to moss for lining hanging baskets, or use the moss you have raked from the lawn. Prunings can be made into compost and cut willow and bamboo canes make great plant supports. Bundle up the hollow

SELECTING RECLAIMED TIMBER

- ☐ Flaky paint adds interest, especially if the undercoat and topcoat are different colours and plenty of wood is showing through.

- ☐ Hammer old nails into the timber, rather than removing them – the rusty tops will increase the individuality of the wood.

- ☐ Sun-bleached wood has a beautiful, shiny, pewter finish to it.

- ☐ Old pallets are covered with dents and scrapes, which gives them their character. If you can't find any old wood, age some new timber by beating it with a chain.

- ☐ Do not choose wood that snaps easily or has large swirls (a loose grain), which means it is too soft and will rot quickly.

stems of several bamboo canes to make a home for insects, while seedheads, such as teasel, make super homemade decorations.

■ **Out and about.** Collect leaves from the side of the road to make leaf mould, seaweed for mulching cabbage, and driftwood or old rope from the beach to make sculptures and unusual plant supports.

■ **From the sky.** Don't miss the opportunity to catch rainwater. Attach a water butt to your shed at the allotment, especially if your site doesn't have water on tap, to collect rainwater from guttering and greenhouse roofs (see p. 178).

■ **Farms and stables.** Manure and mushroom compost are two of the best soil improvers; source them from an organic grower if you can (see p.84 and p.88). Use straw to mulch the fruit patch.

■ **The kitchen.** Olive oil cans and old, cracked crockery make unusual and interesting plant containers. Coffee grindings work well as a dark mulch and will keep the slugs off your precious plants. Old fridges and freezers, provided they have had the CFC removed, make a good, mice-free store for seeds and

tip

Many coffee shops will be happy to let you have their old grindings if you ask, and they might also let you have some of their used plastic coffee cups for raising seedlings in.

harvested vegetables. Either bury them in the ground or hide them beneath a deck. Bottles and jam jars can be used for tea-light holders and to embellish garden walls.

■ **Army surplus shops.** Cargo nets make good climbing nets for kids, and camouflage nets will disguise their dens. Jerry cans can be used to lug water to the allotment, or as industrial-scale water butts, benches or tables – you name it, the army uses it!

■ **Marine salvage yards.** If you're lucky enough to live by the sea, or if you're just visiting on holiday, these are great places for picking up old chains and ropes to use as plant supports, plus anchors, brightly-coloured fenders and lifebuoys for garden decorations.

■ **Microbrewery.** This is a good source of spent hops that can be used for mulches and soil improvers.

■ **Driftwood.** If you live close to the seaside keep an eye out for attractive timber that's washed up on the beach. Its bleached colour and gnarled shapes make beautiful natural sculptures for the garden, as well as mobiles. If you find enough you can even use it for banisters and furniture. In my garden I used a series of pieces screwed together to make a divide between the top and second terrace to stop my toddler daughter falling off the edge. I also combined it with an old pallet I had to make a bench (see p.238).

USING NATIVE TIMBER AND PLANT MATERIALS

I love using native timber and plants instead of imported materials. They look so much better in the garden, and half the fun is sourcing them and then turning them into something practical and attractive; whether it is a prop for a floppy peony or a piece of furniture made from reclaimed timber.

PEA-STICKS AS PLANT SUPPORTS

I like using sticks as plant supports. They might not last as long as plastic props, but they are far more pleasurable to work with and look better too. You can use almost any twiggy deciduous plant, but the traditional choices are birch and hazel cut into 90cm (3ft) lengths.

Birch is particularly good for propping up herbaceous flowers, as the twigs grow in fronds that lend support by leaning against the flowers and creating a natural look. Push them into the ground around topple-prone plants as they start to grow in spring and the birch twigs will keep the plants upright through to autumn.

Hazel is twiggy and particularly good for heavy-duty jobs, such as supporting delphiniums and providing a climbing frame for peas and beans. Push the twigs into the ground and plait and tie the bendy twigs at the top together for extra strength.

NATURAL POLES

Chestnut and hazel poles, gathered from woodlands, have long been used to make garden structures, such as bean wigwams, hurdle fences and natural arbours. Not everyone has the space to grow his or her own, but you have to know where to shop to buy them as they are not sold in garden centres. I get mine from local woodland trusts or tree surgeons. The best time to buy is in autumn and winter, when the trees can be cut to order. During spring woodlands are often left undisturbed while birds are nesting. Also, wood cut when the sap is rising in the spring is prone to sprout leaves, which, although not damaging, wilt and look unsightly.

LEFT: Old Chinese proverb: a few peasticks around your dahlias in spring will save cursing over broken flower stems come summer.

MAKE A SWEET PEA WIGWAM

A sweet pea wigwam is dead easy to make from five hazel poles 2.1m (7ft) long. Firstly, mark a 70cm (28in) circle in the soil. Following the circle, push the poles into the soil making sure they are evenly spaced. Lash the tops of the poles together with twine and either weave a spiral of more twine down the sides, or use willow wands for a more permanent effect.

If you choose to use willow, plait two stems together, to make the structure strong, and either use living willow or pre-soaked dead willow for flexibility. Introduce new willow wands as you go up the structure and cut off any loose ends; wrap more wands around the top to hide the twine lashing the poles together. Thicken up the sides by weaving in more willow around the plaited wands.

WILLOW

There are many specialist willow or 'withy' growers who supply dozens of species for basket-making and garden work. Many sell ready-made kits for building living tunnels and arbours, as well as the usual bundles for your own use. The most common willow for garden use is *Salix viminalis*, a green, bendy species that can be used for everything from staking plants to making wigwams, hurdles and even living structures such as domes and tunnels.

When you buy willow depends on what you want to make. If you are making a living structure that is rooted in situ and leafs up through the growing season to make a dense shape, you need to buy the willow in the dormant season. Dry willow can be bought year-round, but it is dead and won't ever grow. This is an advantage if you want to use it to stake plants, as living willow would soon start to grow and compete with the plants it is supposed to be staking. Dry willow can be woven, but it needs to be soaked in water for a few days beforehand. This makes it as flexible and tough as leather, so it can be plaited and woven into plant supports and sculptures and left to dry.

Dry willow can only be wetted once, so only soak what you need and leave the rest in the shed where it will keep indefinitely. Soak the thicker ends for three days then turn them round to do the tops for two more days.

tip

Willow whips come in different sizes and are sold by the bolt – a tightly bound bundle of stems 30cm (12in) across, so the thinner the stems the more of them you get.

UNDERSTANDING SOIL

In its natural state soil will only support a limited number of plants – if you want your garden to work harder you will need to add outsourced soil improvers. Most garden soils are what is known as 'loam', which contains a mixture of sand, clay, silt and humus (broken down organic matter).

Of course, few soils have the perfect balance of these ingredients. Some contain more clay, which makes them heavy and hard to dig; some have more sand, which makes them drain freely, washes out nutrients and makes them prone to drying out; other soils may also have lots of stony flint or chalk. Whatever your soil type, however, over time it can be improved.

In order to make your soil better, you need to understand what is in it. Take a crumbly clod of earth in your hand. The soil you are holding is alive, at least half its weight is made up of a variety of living organisms that help to make plants grow vigorously.

Fungi in the soil, called mycorrhizae, connect and enter the roots of plants to feed on the complex mixture of sugars in the plant's sap – this isn't a problem for the plant, as the sugars are easily replaced. As the fungi gorge on the sugar they grow rapidly and absorb salts, minerals and water from the soil. Most of these nutrients are superfluous to the fungi and are passed on to the plant, so in a nutshell the plants are trading sugar for nutrients and water with organisms that also vastly increase the working area of the plant's roots.

Other soil-dwelling organisms help plants by releasing nutrients from dead leaves and dung. There are thousands of types of soil bacteria, adapted to different soil conditions that turn organic waste into humus-rich soil using enzymes. Earthworms do their part by breaking the soil down into a crumbly, workable tilth.

The more organisms – fungal mycorrhizae, beneficial bacteria and earthworms – that are present in the soil, the healthier your plants will be. And the best way to increase their numbers is to regularly add compost or soil improver to your garden soil.

GARDEN COMPOST

The time-honoured way of making your beds and borders as naturally nutrient-rich and moisture-retentive as possible is by making and forking in garden compost. It is also great for solving soil problems, such as too free-draining and heavy, sticky soil.

Almost anything that is made from organic material – plants, paper, and food scraps (not meat) – will break down into garden compost. The art of composting in the garden is all about making these things break down as quickly and consistently as possible into a crumbly, weed-free, sweet-smelling soil improver that plants will love. And it can be very absorbing – I've gone from ignoring the great green monster at the bottom of the garden to looking forward to making compost.

There are two types of compost heap: hot heaps that rot down quickly and cool heaps that need a year or two to mature.

HOT HEAPS

When bacteria start to break down organic matter they generate energy in the form of heat, which is what causes the compost heap to steam like a volcano. Hot heaps create the best compost as the heat kills weed seeds and the results are quick. The key to success is using the right mix of material – nitrogen-rich fresh grass clippings and kitchen scraps or fresh manure mixed 50/50 with carbon-rich scrunched up newspaper, fallen leaves, hedge clippings and spent flower stems. Sprinkle it with a can of water if the mix is dry and fill the compost bin in one go, or at least in layers 30cm (12in) deep or more.

Within a few days the mix will heat up and start to steam. When steam stops coming out of the top of the compost bin, after about four weeks, empty the whole lot out, mix it together, add more water if it is dry and re-fill the compost bin. 'Turning' allows in more air that kick-starts the bacteria responsible for the hot composting process.

When no more heat is being produced after turning (after 8–10 weeks), leave the compost to mature for a few weeks. You can tell it is ready when the ingredients have broken down into an odourless, dark mass. In summer, when the weather is warm, good garden compost can be ready for use in as little as six weeks!

tip

You cannot use garden compost for potting up plants or sowing seeds, as it does not have the right mixture of nutrients and texture and it is not sterile enough for seeds.

Put a lid on your compost bin to stop it getting sodden and therefore slow to rot.

TIPS FOR YOUR CLASSIC PALLET COMPOST BIN

■ Mesh on the inside of your heap will prevent animals such as hedgehogs from hibernating amongst the collected clippings and being disturbed if the contents are turned. It will also keep pests, such as mice and rats, out.

■ Cover your compost with a lid so heavy rain does not soak the mix. A plastic sheet held down with bricks will do.

■ Position the heap over bare soil so that water can drain away.

■ Build the heap in sun or semi-shade, and near a water supply so that you can keep the contents moist. Moisture will speed up the composting of dry material and deter wasps and ants from setting up home in the heap.

■ Add water if the compost is dry or newspaper if it is wet.

The best compost comes from a mix of materials – green stuff for nitrogen and brown for carbon.

COMPOST TROUBLE SHOOTER

Q: Grass clippings are turning into a stinky slime.
A: Keep a stack of newspaper or shredded woodchips by the compost heap to blend with and bulk up the contents of the mower box.

Q: What do I do with diseased plant materials?
A: By autumn some leaves will show the silvery sheen of mildew or spots and blotches caused by fungal diseases. These diseases won't spread in the finished compost, as friendly microbes, even in a cool heap, will kill them off, so push them deep into the centre of the compost heap. Soil-borne diseases that suddenly kill or stunt plants out of season are a different matter and plants suffering from these should not be composted. As a general rule of thumb, if you are not sure, burn it.

Q: There are un-composted bits in the finished compost.
A: Small twigs won't be a problem, and can be spread or used to improve the soil before planting as normal. Larger pieces and stems should be chopped up with a spade and added back to the heap.

TO COMPOST OR NOT TO COMPOST?

Not everything is good for your compost heap. These lists show you what you can and cannot add:

Yes:
- Grass clippings, mix with scrunched sheets of newspaper for best results.
- Easy to pull up annual weeds.
- Autumn leaves.
- Herbaceous plant stems.
- Bedding plants that have caught the frost.
- Newspaper, scrunched up into balls.
- Paper and envelopes – best shredded.
- Cardboard, torn up.
- Bedding from herbivorous pets, such as rabbits and hamsters.
- Vegetable peelings from the kitchen.
- Shredded wood and hedge clippings.
- Tea bags, eggshells, coffee grounds.

No:
- Glossy magazines – recycle instead.
- Cooked food – even cooked vegetables go slimy and make turning unpleasant.
- Meat, bones or fish.
- Cat litter or dog faeces.
- Plastic.
- Large twigs or branches.
- Large pieces of timber.
- Diseased plants that are infected with soil-borne diseases, such as club root on cabbage.
- Perennial weed roots and weed seeds, although these can be hot composted.

COOL HEAPS

Cool heaps are less effort. Like the hot heap, the cold heap is a repository for all garden and leafy kitchen waste, but it can be added to a cool heap as and when the waste becomes available – although the more blended nitrogen and carbon-rich material you can add in one go, the better. Because waste is added piecemeal the composting bacteria and earthworms work at a steady pace, but occasional turning (mixing together) with a fork will help to speed things up. Turning is also a good opportunity to water any dry material or to add newspaper to soak up any excess moisture from the mix.

tip

I make a point of turning my cool heaps at least twice a year – once in the winter, after the big autumn clear up, and once in late summer. This is when I can harvest some finished compost from the bottom of the heap for autumn mulching and digging, and to make room for the autumn rush.

OTHER SOIL IMPROVERS

If you don't have room for a composter, or can't produce enough to fulfil your needs, a range of soil improvers are available from various other sources.

GREEN COMPOST

This is the composted remains of leaves and plants that are collected by the council or left by gardeners at green waste collection points. The availability and quality can be variable, depending on where you live, but in general it is brilliant stuff and can be bought economically either bagged or by the trailer-load.

It is low in nutrients and bulky, which makes it ideal for helping dry soils to hold on to moisture and wet soils to become freer draining, and because it has been composted at extremely high temperatures it is completely weed and disease free. The only downside for some is that it is very fine and tends to stain your hands, so wear gloves if this bothers you.

Dig it into the soil like garden compost, or use as a mulch. It's black colour will give a smart finish to bare soil in beds and borders and will help to warm the soil in vegetable beds in the spring. I use it mixed 50/50 with garden soil for filling raised beds and blend about a third green compost to two thirds potting compost to save money when filling large containers.

tip

THE COMPOST CONE
As well as the pallet compost bins that I have on my allotment, I think the 'plastic cone' composters that you can buy from garden centres are also excellent. They are great for 'hot' composting, as they hold in the heat, and are also good for storing leaf-mould and pungent manure. If you are starting an allotment or a new garden, cones are just the thing for dealing with 'nasties' such as weed seeds and roots.

If there's one thing I've learned about collected seaweed, it's that it's smelly, so never put it in the back of your wife's car.

COCOA SHELLS

These chocolate-smelling husks come from cocoa beans and can be dangerous for dogs, so don't use them if you share your garden with one. Cocoa shells are, however, a brilliant weed suppressant as the angular husks lock together and they don't blow around in the breeze. This material costs three times as much as bark chippings, but it makes a good slug and snail deterrent, as they don't like crossing it, so perhaps reserve it for vulnerable plants, such as hostas, newly planted dahlias and young perennials in spring.

MUSHROOM COMPOST

Spent mushroom compost is a waste product from mushroom farms. It is an economical soil improver to buy and can be used for digging in and mulching. It is made from blended poultry manure, chalk and composted straw and can be as much as 30 per cent chalk, which makes it alkaline and unsuitable for use around ericaceous plants such as rhododendrons that require acidic soil, or blueberries that prefer neutral or acid conditions. It is great for vegetables, however, and for 'sweetening' acidic soils. Some garden centres do sell it, or look online for a local mushroom producer. Before using it remove any large lumps of chalk, and don't be alarmed if a crop of edible mushrooms appears from your mulch in the autumn!

SEAWEED

Collect seaweed for free from slipways or from the beach after a storm. The time to collect is from autumn, through winter, to spring – after this it can be a bit too smelly and full of flies to put in the back of the car! Collect it when it is fresh and wet as it will be less salty than dry weed that has been sitting on the beach in the salt-laden breeze.

I use it for vegetables, putting a bucket or two in bean and potato trenches before planting, and as a mulch around winter cabbages as the dry, crispy weed keeps slugs at bay. It is also good as nutrient-rich filler for the compost heap.

COMPOSTED BARK OR WOODCHIPS

Tree surgeons sell this and it can be very economical to buy. It has low levels of nutrients, but is ideal for digging in to improve drainage in heavy soils. It is also good for piling onto newspaper around plants to create a weed-suppressing layer.

SPENT HOPS

A by-product from the brewing industry, spent hops are flowers from the climbing hop plant which, because of their essential oils, are steeped in beer to add flavour. Once their work at the brewery is done they are bagged up and dumped, but if you can get hold of them at this stage they make a great mulch or soil improver, particularly for crops such as onions and fruit (blueberries in particular) that like acid soils. Try to avoid letting it get into contact with the collars of your plants, though, as it can cause scorching.

Although they don't need composting, hops make a good compost accelerator and will speed up the rotting process when added to a heap. If you own a dog, only use hops on the compost heap, as they will gorge themselves on any fresh hops that are spread around plants and make themselves very ill. Source spent hops from local breweries… along with some local beer!

tip

The fibrous nature of hops means that they come into their own as a soil conditioner, and if you don't like the smell of beer the sweet scent soon disappears.

MAKE A COMFREY FEEDER

Comfrey (*Symphytum*) is a living plant-food factory. Its lengthy roots prospect for nutrients deep in the soil, which are then stored in its leaves. Simply steeping the leaves in water for 4–6 weeks will yield a potash-rich liquid that is ideal for feeding flowering and fruiting plants, such as tomatoes. The only downside is that the liquid is very smelly, so I prefer to crush the nutrient-rich juice straight from the leaves and keep it in a sealed container.

Buy a piece of pipe 10cm (4in) in diameter and 1.2m (4ft) long and an end-cap – you can often get free off-cuts from builders or you can buy it from builders' merchants. Glue the end-cap onto one end (1) and drill a 5mm ($^1/_4$in) hole through the end-cap to allow the juice to run out (2). Attach the pipe vertically to your shed or greenhouse with plastic gutter clips (3) and pack the pipe with freshly cut comfrey leaves (4) (you can also use young nettles if they are cut in the spring). Weigh the leaves down with a fizzy drink bottle filled with sand. Tie a sturdy piece of string around the top of the bottle so that it can be pulled out and the pipe reloaded with more leaves (5).

After a few weeks black juice will start to drip out of the hole in the end-cap. Collect it in a pot (6) and dilute it with 1:10 parts water. It can be stored in a clearly marked bottle for use later the same season.

tip

The best type of comfrey plant to choose is non-spreading, non-flowering 'Bocking 14'.

1

4

2
3

5
6

MANURE

Manure is the traditional and best way of increasing soil fertility. All manures must be well rotted for at least six months before you use them on the soil, as they can scorch plant roots and it is also very smelly! Put fresh manure into an ordinary compost bin, cover it with plastic and leave it to rot down. You will know it is ready to use when the smell of ammonia has been replaced by a nice earthy scent, the straw or woodchips that are in it have broken down, and it has a crumbly texture. It is well worth finding a local supplier, even if you have to follow a horse back to the stables! People are usually only too glad to get rid of the stuff, so chances are you will be able to get it for free, or strike a deal for just the cost of delivery.

tip

Chicken manure is high in nitrogen and boosts foliage, so use it to re-feed soil that has been vacated by hungry, leafy crops, such as cabbages. It is also good for encouraging extra-tall sunflowers, creating a leafy, tropical look with annual castor oil plants, or where you want fast wall-cover from tall annual climbers, such as cathedral bells and canary creeper.

CHICKEN MANURE

If you get this straight from the chicken always wear gloves and wash your hands after handling it, otherwise you can buy it as sterilized pellets in proprietary tubs from the garden centre. The real stuff can be used as a compost accelerator, so if you keep chickens it can go straight onto the compost heap. If you keep it separate it should be stacked up and left for a year to rot. Chicken manure is very high in nitrogen so it is great as a growth-boosting mulch in the spring.

COW AND PIG MANURE

Although it is great for roses, cow and pig manure tends to be very smelly so it is probably best restricted to the allotment, although the smell will deteriorate over time with composting. Cow and pig manure is slightly richer in flower and health-boosting potassium than horse manure, so it is just the thing for outdoor tomatoes, potatoes and prize-winning pumpkins.

HORSE MANURE

This is the most widely available manure, and the most pleasant to handle. It is great for conditioning and improving the texture of soil as it's lightweight and not slimy like pig and cow dung. It works with all types of difficult, unworkable soil and is great for improving fertility in vegetable beds and allotments.

tip

Wear Wellington boots and gloves when dealing with manure.

POTTING COMPOSTS

Composts for potting are normally bought in bags from the garden centre, rather than created at home in heaps, because it is sterile, weed free and has been developed to produce consistent results. The only exception on the homemade front is worm compost (see p.90), but this still needs blending with a proprietary compost to become an enricher for hungry plants, such as pot-grown courgettes and dahlias. The most popular potting compost is multipurpose compost, which can be used for potted patio flowers, vegetable pots and even for sowing seeds.

tip

Multipurpose compost can be bought quite cheaply, but don't just think about price as the quality varies. Try different brands until you find a favourite.

TYPES OF POTTING COMPOST

■ **Multipurpose.** This contains mostly peat, mixed with composted bark and sometimes wood fibre. It is ideal for patio pots, and better than John Innes No 2 or No 3 for hanging baskets and balconies, where weight is an issue. It is also low in nutrients, so it's fine for sowing seeds.

■ **Peat-free multipurpose.** I prefer to use peat-free compost on environmental grounds. It is made up of materials such as green compost, coir and composted bark and is an alternative to peat, which is dug from diminishing peat land habitats that are, amongst other things, home to a host of rare wildlife. Peat-free is heavier than peat-based multipurpose compost, but it is richer in nutrients. Some formulations are very alkaline, so they are unsuitable for ericaceous plants.

■ **Ericaceous.** This is a mixture of loam, peat and grit which is specially formulated for plants that need acidic soil conditions, such as rhododendrons and azaleas. If the soil is too alkaline it causes an iron deficiency that results in yellowing leaves.

■ **John Innes No 1, No 2 and No 3.** More like an ordinary garden soil in texture, John Innes mixes are commonly formulated from loam, grit, peat, lime and fertilizer – there are also an increasing number of

peat-free formulations available. No 1 has the least nutrients, so it is ideal for seed sowing, taking cuttings and potting on small plants. No 2 has slightly more nutrients and No 3 has the most nutrients, both are ideal for pots. I often mix peat-free multipurpose with John Innes composts as it makes the compost easier to re-wet if it dries out and adds a bit of weight to stop top-heavy pots from being blown over.

■ **Grow bags.** These are the traditional bag for growing tomatoes and cucumbers on hot patios where there is no soil. I cut them in half and turn them up on their ends to make deeper compost bags that can be easily disguised inside another pot or old tin can. They are available with peat or peat-free, but in recent trials, peat-free grow bags were found to out-perform peat-based bags.

■ **Container and hanging basket.** These are specifically formulated for hungry bedding and patio plants that flower profusely and need plenty of nutrients. They are more expensive than multipurpose compost due to the added extras, such as wetting agents, slow-release fertilizer and water-retaining crystals. You can, however, make your own container and hanging basket compost by buying peat-free multipurpose compost and customizing it yourself.

WORMERIES

Wormeries are ideal for composting kitchen peelings and limited amounts of garden clippings. They are great if you don't have much space, but still want to compost. You can buy ready-made, indiscreet wormeries that are shaped more like bins and water butts and come with full instructions, but my best wormery was made in an old bath that was hidden behind the shed on the allotment. Granted, not everyone wants an old bathtub in his or her garden, but believe me it makes the ideal worm home.

To get my worms started in their new 'old bath' home, I piled in a few buckets of well-rotted compost then topped up the bath with part-composted manure, sourced from the stacked remains of the hot bed I had made earlier in the year. The manure itself contained so many worms that I needn't have bothered with any extra, but I bunged in around another 1,000 to be sure and then topped off the lot with grass clippings and soft, leafy prunings. Not all types of worm, certainly not big earthworms from the garden, will enjoy the rich conditions inside a wormery, so you need to obtain a litter-dwelling species that naturally makes their home near the soil surface amongst fallen plant debris. Commonly available species including tiger worms (*Eisenia fetida*) and red worms (*Lumbricus rubellus*). To keep hungry blackbirds at bay, I made a cover from some weed-suppressing mat, which also kept out the light while letting the rain in to keep the wormery moist.

I waited a month for the worms to establish then, once they were working right through the mix, I topped up the bath with a steady supply of compostables. Unlike with my previous, shop-bought model, harvesting the processed compost was quite simple and involved concentrating new compostables at one end to draw the worms out of the finished compost, leaving it worm-free for scooping out. In order to collect the rich liquid fertilizer produced by the worms, I simply put a tub under the open plughole to catch it.

tip

Wormeries are brilliant for creating homemade potting compost and liquid feeds – add one part feed to three parts compost for best results.

GET THE BEST FROM YOUR WORMERY

■ **Location.** The best place for a wormery is a sheltered, warm spot out of direct summer sun. Worms process food best when the temperature is 12–23°C (54–73°F), so insulate your wormery with old blankets in cold weather, or if possible move it to the greenhouse in winter.

■ **Check for moisture.** Every so often get a handful of forming compost from the bottom of the wormery and give it a squeeze. If the moisture content is right it should bind together. If it crumbles the compost is too dry, so add water, if lots of water oozes out, cover the top with a plastic sheet to keep out the rain and mix in more newspaper to soak up the excess.

■ **What to put in.** When in full production, worms eat their own body weight in food each day. Avoid putting in meat that may attract vermin and smells as it rots, and acidic foods such as onions and citrus. Add lots of ripped-up newspaper soaked in water – the worms will love it. You might also want to add some worm feed (ground-up grain that fishermen use to fatten up their worms for bait), which is available from angling shops or mail order via the Internet.

■ **Other inhabitants.** Compost or fruit flies often take up residence in a wormery, but you can reduce the numbers of maggots by adding a few pinches of garden lime (available from garden centres) every fortnight to keep the compost sweet. Also net the top to keep out flies.

■ **Mould.** This develops when more food goes into the wormery than the worms can eat. It won't harm the worms, just cut back on the amount you are putting in.

GROWING YOUR GARDEN

PART TWO

GROWING FROM SEEDS, STEMS AND ROOTS

Sowing seeds is one of my favourite gardening tasks. I love the process of filling pots with compost, gently taking the seeds from their packets and sprinkling them on the soil. It is a mesmerizing process, and I can get lost for hours sowing just a few packets. The seeds themselves are fascinating too – each plant family has its own type, and individual varieties of plant are often distinguishable by their seeds alone. Spring onion seeds are the shape and colour of black volcanic sand, while the seeds of the cabbage family are reminiscent of shotgun pellets. Cucumbers and pumpkins, on the other hand, look like miniature hot-water bottles. Every seed contains a root – or radicle – to prospect for moisture, and tiny 'seed leaves' that will grow towards the light.

COMPOST FOR SEEDS

Seeds need moisture to germinate, which is where potting compost comes in. Designed to hold water like a sponge, but without drowning seedlings or becoming stagnant, the open structure of particles in potting compost allow young roots to burrow and establish. Composts that are specifically blended for seed sowing are usually made up of peat, composted bark or coir, plus some sand to enhance drainage. Some gardeners swear by peat-based composts for sowing seeds, but it is a controversial issue because the digging up of peat for use in horticulture damages precious and rare natural habitats. Wherever possible I suggest using peat-free composts.

Whether you choose to use peat or peat-free compost it will be sterile, which means establishing seeds won't have to compete with disease and weeds as they grow. Seed compost contains very little plant food as seeds need no nutrients to sprout, in fact, if they're sown in a pot that is too nutrient-rich it can affect germination. Multipurpose composts are the 'Jack of all trades' in the world of compost. They can be used for sowing as they don't contain much plant food, but they can also be topped up with fertilizer in the growing season for larger plants.

9cm plastic pots
are perfect for
seeds and cuttings.

CONTAINERS

The range of containers that are available for sowing seeds increases every year, but what you use largely comes down to what you are growing. Most containers are made of plastic. It pays to spend more on quality pots that can be relied on to give a few seasons of service, rather than cheap, flimsy versions that will crack and need replacing every spring.

Some gardeners recycle old plastic coffee cups, mushroom boxes and tin cans. This is fine if you are a sporadic sower, and I'm all for recycling, but there are drawbacks. Often the sizes don't match, which can make potting less convenient, and they can quickly deteriorate in bright sunlight, plus I think they look somewhat untidy piled up under the potting bench.

We use a staggering 500 million plastic plant pots in the UK each year. If you are keen to use less plastic (and who isn't?) the latest trend is to use pots made from natural plant starches, including rice, bamboo and corn. Unlike their plastic counterparts, after a few years of service they rot away to nothing.

POTS

■ I use 10cm (4in) pots for most seeds. They are wide enough at the rim to allow for up to 20 medium-sized seeds, such as tomatoes, to be sown, pricked out (see page 102) and potted up individually. They are also the best size for sowing larger, fast growing seeds, such as sunflowers, pumpkins and sweet peas, that are sown singly and do not need pricking out as they are simply potted on or planted out.

■ The perfect size for potting up seedlings that like room to grow, and stay in their pots until they are ready for planting out after the frosts, are 8cm (3in) pots. I use them for flowers with spreading leaves, such as tomatoes and chilli peppers. It's easy to pack a lot of these pots onto a windowsill or potting bench.

■ Trays of square, punnet-shaped pots, or cells, that are joined together are known as cell trays. They make moving a lot of plants around much easier and are a great way to raise vegetables, particularly crops that need to be grown in large quantities, such as lettuce, kohl rabi and leeks. The individual cells that make up the cell trays come in a range of sizes, from 12cm (5in) to 2cm (¾in). Choose your cell trays according to the seeds you are sowing: 2cm (¾in) cells for thin, upright leeks and spring onions; 8cm (3in) cells for slender French beans; and 12cm (5in) cells for broad-shouldered crops, such as cabbages.

■ Paper pots are easy to make, eco-friendly and economical. Unlike normal pots, plants can be left in paper pots when they are planted out in the garden as the paper gradually breaks down in the soil. Use paper pots for flowers such as poppies that hate having their roots disturbed. Because the height of these pots can be customized to make taller pots, I use them for crops such as peas that have deep roots. They also come in handy when all of my plastic pots are in use. Here's how to make one…

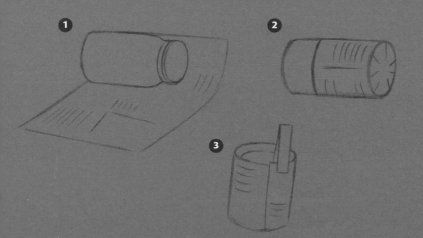

1 Fold a sheet of newspaper in half, and half again until it is 10–15cm (4–6in) tall, then loosely roll it around an open-ended glass jar.

2 Scrunch the excess paper at the end into the bottom of the jar to make a base.

3 Slide the jar out of the paper, and staple the sides together. Then you can fill it with compost, and water well before sowing your seeds.

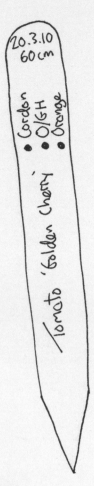

LABELS

Labels are for more than just plant names – much more! Labels are an *aide-mémoire* for all the information on the seed packet – information about the colour, size or spread of a plant which may prove to be invaluable later on. It also pays to add the sowing date, so you don't keep tending seeds for months after they've given up the ghost.

PREPARING POTS FOR SOWING

Fill each pot to the brim with compost then, rather than packing it down, tap the base of the pots on your table or bench to settle the compost down. Brush any extra compost off the top with the side of your hand and give the pots a good watering, until the water flows out of the holes in the bottom. This will reduce the height of the compost to just below the rim, for easy watering later, and will settle the particles so that they are touching one another but are not so packed that air is excluded (roots need air to breathe). After leaving the pots to stand for five minutes, start sowing.

One piece of kit that I've learnt to keep in my greenhouse is a pair of scissors. For years, I'd tear into the seed packets and, although it was the fastest way of getting at the seeds, the dirty, ripped packets made it difficult to read the instructions and hard to store extra seeds for later use. These days I take a far more careful approach and diligently cut the top off seed packets with scissors.

tip

Pencil is the best weatherproof marker for labels, and far outlasts so-called permanent markers. The best type is a 'carpenter's pencil' that can be bought from hardware stores. Make your own labels from old lolly sticks or cut them out of a used plastic carton.

WHAT, WHEN AND WHERE TO SOW

■ **What.** If you haven't sown annuals (plants that live and flower for just one year), you'll be amazed at how easy they are to grow. They should be sown in spring to flower in the summer. My favourites include marigolds, love-in-a-mist, cosmos and Californian poppies. Biennials (plants that live for two years and flower in the second year), such as foxgloves and sweet Williams, are sown between spring and midsummer, planted out in the autumn and flower from spring the following year. Many perennials (plants that flower every year) can also be grown from seed. Particularly rewarding are those that flower in their first year, such as lupins, aquilegia and verbena, and quick-to-grow ornamental grasses, such as stipa and miscanthus. Turn to the Edible Garden chapter (p.120) for vegetables that can be grown from seed.

■ **When.** Spring is the traditional time for sowing, ideally from March to May, but always check the seed packets because planting times for seeds vary.

■ **Where.** Depending on what you are sowing, either sow in compost-filled pots or seed trays, or sow the seeds directly into the soil where you want the flowers to grow. Most seeds need warmth and sunshine to sprout and grow, so for those sown in pots a sunny windowsill or greenhouse is ideal.

SEEDS

Whether carefully cut open or hastily ripped into, once the seeds are liberated from their packets their size is the first clue as to how to treat them…

SMALL SEEDS

By small, I mean dust-like. The group of plants that come from small seeds includes many garden favourites, such as begonias, Busy Lizzies, lobelia and petunias. As the seeds are so small their resources are limited, and they don't have enough stored energy to push up through soil or compost to sprout. If they are buried, they will lie dormant until they become exposed to the sun.

Because this type of seed needs to lie on the surface of the compost in order to sprout, the key to success is to ensure that your compost is watered before sowing. I find the easiest way to sow them is in small trays.

MEDIUM SEEDS

Most seeds can be categorized as medium-sized, including sand-like spring onion seeds, the tufted tubes of French marigolds and the pale pips of tomatoes. Before sowing, water the soil and allow it to drain. Medium seeds prefer to be buried so that moisture in the surrounding soil will soak into their thicker seed coats and soften them.

Medium seeds should be buried to twice their depth, so the larger the seed the deeper it needs to go. Cover the planted seeds by sieving compost over the top of them. This process gets rid of any larger particles of compost that could smother the seeds before they have a chance to sprout. If, like me, you don't have a sieve, just use another pot instead. Half-fill it with compost and gently shake so that a layer of fine compost falls out of the holes in the bottom and just covers your seeds.

Be careful, though, it is easy to over-sow medium-sized seed, which means sowing too many in a pot. For one thing, it is a waste of money as crowded seeds always become long and spindly as they compete in the close quarters for light. It is far better to sow another pot and give your seeds plenty of space, rather than packing them like sardines.

I always use 10cm (4in) pots, tapping the seed from the packet and spreading any clumps with my finger. They don't need to be evenly spaced, but try to avoid letting them sit on top of each other. The number of seeds depends on the type of seed you are sowing. If you want a lot of flowers, sow 20–30 seeds to a 10cm (4in) pot, or for even larger numbers use a tray – prick the seedlings out as soon as they are large enough to handle to avoid overcrowding. For expensive seeds, such as F1 chilli peppers and tomatoes (see page 103), only sow enough seeds for the number of plants you want to grow, and a couple for luck, though in truth F1 seeds are so reliable that they are almost guaranteed to sprout.

LARGE SEEDS

Large seeds, such as sunflowers, pumpkins, courgettes and peas, are child's play to sow. They need little more than gently pushing into damp compost, either individually or in pairs, in 8cm (3in) pots to twice the depth of the seed. The idea of pushing

tip

If you struggle with seeing small seeds, mix them in a bowl with dry sand first – the sand makes handling and spreading the seeds evenly far easier. Never water newly sown small seeds from above, as even a gentle sprinkle will have them surfing to the sides of the trays where they'll fight for space.

tip

Store seeds in a cool, dry place; a plastic tub with a re-sealable lid is ideal. If left out in the open and stuck behind pots in the greenhouse, shed or cupboard, they will soon lose their viability in the damp air.

RIGHT: Mixed packets of seed, for example sunflowers of different colours, will contain seeds of various sizes and colours. To ensure you get the full range of flowers, identify and sow a few of each type.

two seeds into each pot is a belts-and-braces technique to ensure you get at least one plant if the other should fail. If both seeds germinate, pinch out the weaker seedling, but don't pull it out, as this will disturb the roots of its neighbour.

PRICKING OUT

This simply means moving seedlings from the pot where they were sown into individual containers to grow on. When a seed sprouts, the first pair of leaves it produces are called 'seed leaves'. Like flat-pack foliage, these leaves already exist inside the seed, but because these pioneer leaves have to fit inside the seed they are a different shape to the adult or true leaves that grow later. As the seed germinates, the newly spreading roots draw in moisture from the soil and the seed leaves fill out, grow, and start drawing energy from the sun. Each type of plant has its own distinctive seed leaves, which is a useful way to identify them if the label has been lost, and also for distinguishing crops from weeds.

To prevent root damage I prefer to knock clumps of seedlings out of the tray before pricking them out individually into pots.

F1 SEED

F1 does not mean 'Formula One', although much like the supercharged racing cars these plants could be described as thoroughbred. F1 in plant terms stands for 'first filial generation', which means that the plant is the result of a series of intricate cross-pollinations.

In nature, plants spread their pollen far and wide in order to pollinate with the widest number of plant partners. This ensures the genetic properties of each plant are carried into the next generation and beyond. When plant breeders create F1s they turn this natural pollination process on its head by restricting generations of plants to interbreeding, which creates unhealthy plants that lack vigour. The last cross in the process is made with a completely different plant variety from a different gene pool. This creates 'the first filial generation', which, like an angry teenager, rebels against its lacklustre parents and becomes super robust. The process of creating F1 plants – the hand pollination and double, triple and quadruple crossing – is reflected in the price of the seeds and the small amount you get in each packet.

Key characteristics of F1 seeds are better germination rates, uniform growth, increased ability to shrug off pests and diseases, and regular cropping times. Many would argue that this uniformity is fine for flowers, but not so useful when vegetable crops all ripen at the same time and create gluts.

The time to prick out seedlings is when the seed leaves are large enough to hold by one leaf between your finger and thumb. Very small seeds, such as lobelia, are too tiny to hold by a single leaf. Rather than try with tweezers, knock them out of their pots or tray and re-pot a pinch of seedlings at a time. It might seem counterintuitive to sow seeds en masse into one pot and then move them, one-by-one, to new pots, but it does make sense as it is more space efficient, uses less potting compost and small seeds sprout much better when they are sown together. It also allows you to select the best seedlings for growing on.

tip

Don't water seedlings immediately before pricking them out as the moisture will make the compost heavy and increase the likelihood of snapping their delicate roots.

WATERING

Like all newborns, it is best to keep your seedlings in as clean and sterile living quarters as possible. Sterile potting compost, instead of garden soil, is a must. Keep it moist with tap water – collected rainwater should only be used for more robust, established plants. Once seedlings start to sprout, it is essential to keep the surface of the compost moist. Rather than use a watering can, which will slosh seedlings out of the pot, use a hand mister.

tip

Avoid transplanting seedlings in very hot conditions; if necessary, move them into the shade so the seedlings don't wilt.

PRICKING OUT STEP-BY-STEP

Prepare the pots the seedlings are being moved to by filling them with moist compost. The compost needs to be moist enough so that when you squeeze it in your hand it holds together in a ball. In the centre of the pot, push a short length of bamboo, or your finger, into the compost to make a hole three-quarters of the pot deep.

If just a few seeds have sprouted, hold on to a seed leaf of one of the seedlings and use a short bamboo cane to dig under it and lever it up and out from the pot. Never touch the stem of a seedling as they can be easily bruised, which weakens and can even kill young plants. If there are a lot of seedlings in the pot, gently tip the compost and the seedlings out into a tray. If the compost doesn't split apart, crack it open with your fingers and peel the healthiest seedlings off, again holding them by a single seed leaf.

The best seedlings aren't always the largest. Choose ones that have short stems and a stocky shape, with all their roots and leaves intact. Some will inevitably get broken during the move; if this happens, throw out the damaged seedling and any sentimental thought of keeping it. It sounds tough, but you should only prick out the best plants.

When the roots of the seedling are free from the old soil, move it to the new pot and drop the roots into the prepared hole. Static can cause the roots to snag on the sides of the hole, so I first rub my bamboo cane against my trousers to 'charge' it so that the roots are drawn to the bamboo instead of the sides of the hole. With the roots stuck to the end of the bamboo cane it is easier to guide them down into the bottom of the hole. If the roots bend back on themselves halfway into the hole, remove the seedling, make the hole a little bigger and try again.

With two fingers – one on either side of the seedling – gently firm the seedling into the new compost at the same level it was growing before it was moved. This isn't always easy, but if you initially put your seedling in a little deeper, you can't go wrong. Water the seedlings using a can with a very fine rose (sprinkler) and keep them indoors in a warm, bright and sheltered place.

HARDENING OFF

When plants have been grown inside they need time to acclimatize to cooler temperatures before they are planted outside. This process is called 'hardening off'.

Plant stems only get tough enough to cope with a breeze if they are rocked about; otherwise they stay soft and are prone to snapping when planted outside. Start to harden off seedlings when they are small by occasionally brushing the palm of your hand gently over the tops of the plants – this gentle rocking will trigger wind-resistant growth in the stems.

If you have only raised a few plants inside, put the pots into trays so that you can move them around more easily. Move the plants to a sheltered bright spot outside during the day, and take them back inside at night. After a week, if the weather is mild, leave them outside against a warm sheltered wall for the night – after a week of this they will be ready for planting outside in the garden. If you are raising a lot of plants, a cold frame (see p. 182) is invaluable. This small greenhouse with a lift-up, transparent lid, can be use to harden off plants in situ by incrementally opening the lid to gently acclimatize them to life outside. If a cold or rainy snap interrupts this process, just close the lid to protect the young plants from the worst of the weather.

Sometimes you may find yourself with so many plants that you don't have enough trays or cold frames to cope with them all. In the spring, when my greenhouse is heaving with pots, I break all the rules about hardening off and transplant straight out into the garden where I want them to grow. Rather than leave them to the elements, however, I use sheets of horticultural fleece (see p. 227) to shade and keep them warm. This technique is particularly useful for pot-grown tender crops that take up lots of space inside, such as courgettes, sweet corn and French beans. Use bricks to hold the fleece down, and sticks pushed into the soil to keep the fabric off the leaves. Scatter organic slug-pellets around the still-soft plants, and after a week, if the weather is getting warmer, remove the fleece during the day and cover if the nights are cold (less than 10 °C (50 °F) or windy. After a fortnight, remove the fleece altogether.

RIGHT: 'Now, where to put these tomatoes?' Baker's trays make useful tools for shuffling plants in and out of the greenhouse while you're hardening off your tender crops and flowers in early spring.

SOWING DIRECTLY OUTSIDE

Sowing seed straight into the soil often requires a leap of faith. But if the soil is prepared in the right way and steps are taken to keep natural predators – birds, voles, mice, slugs and snails – at bay there is very little that can go wrong.

SOIL PREPARATION

Firstly, the soil needs to be prepared. Pull out all the weeds, with their roots, from newly created borders and fork the soil through to 'open it up' and break up compacted areas that would otherwise check young roots. Forking through also evens out the soil so that all areas soak up moisture or drain evenly. This is important to ensure that seeds sprout and grow at the same rate, and you are not left with bare patches.

FERTILIZERS

When you are feeding new and existing beds, the type of fertilizer depends on what you are growing. Some plants, such as sweet rocket and Californian poppies, don't need any kind of feed as it encourages large, leafy plants that are reluctant to flower and slower to produce seed.

In general, though, if you want to grow armfuls of annual cut flowers or borders full of bedding plants, add an organic fertilizer that is relatively low in nitrogen to the soil before you sow your seeds. This type of fertilizer is often described as a balanced feed. It contains equal percentages of the three main plant foods: nitrogen (N) for leaves; phosphate (P) for roots; and potassium (K) for general health. Balanced feed helps to boost growth and gives the plants the resources to flower without over-loading them, so that they don't produce excessive leafy growth at the expense of blooms.

Buy granules, as opposed to liquid feed, and spread them over the soil to the rate recommended on the box. As a rough guide, I was taught to work on the principle that a handful of Growmore (the classic general feed formulation) was enough to scatter over $1m^2$ ($1.2 yd^2$) of soil. These days, with so many feeds of so many weights and sizes, it is best to take a slightly more scientific approach. Before using a brand of feed for the first time, I weigh

out the amount needed to cover $1m^2$ ($1.2 \, yd^2$) on the kitchen scales. For the sake of hygiene, pour the feed into a plastic bag to keep it off the scales, tie up the bag and keep it inside the box as a visual guide for when you are next feeding your plants.

Spinach seedlings.

The ideal time for granular feeds is either just before sowing, or when the plants are growing fast in the spring and summer months. If you feed in late autumn and winter, plants will flush with new growth that will be turned to mush by the first cold snap.

WHY SOW ANNUAL FLOWERS?

There is more reason to grow plants from seed than simply to save money. Plants raised from a packet of seeds can achieve things that ready-grown greenery cannot.

FILL A BIG SPACE FAST

Seed-sown annual flowers can completely fill an empty border with flowers in a single summer. Simply scatter the seed of annuals such as larkspur and cornflower in the spring and they will paint your border with swathes of colour by summer. You can also get a far greater range of shapes and colours from annuals, and they are the perfect plants for covering bare soil between newly planted herbaceous flowers and woody shrubs while they are still filling out. Rudbeckias, cosmos and marigolds all form stocky stems that create the illusion of permanence. If you want really broad-shouldered space fillers, sweet peas and multi-stemmed sunflowers such as 'Vanilla Ice' will cover the ground fast.

LEFT: Pride of place in my garden last year was this unusual Dahlia *coccinea* var. *palmeri*. It grows to 8ft tall if tubers are left in the ground over winter and protected with a deep mulch to keep off the cold and rain.

Nasturtiums are versatile annuals that look great in pots and borders, and they're tasty in a salad, too.

KEEP PESTS AT BAY

Attract aphid-eating hoverflies by sowing marigolds and poached egg plants around your vegetable beds. These striped flies look like small wasps, but they don't sting, and they hover like helicopters. They are attracted to yellow flowers to collect nectar, and while they are hovering amongst the flowers they also keep a lookout for aphids – those nasty sapsuckers that can ruin a crop if left unchecked. If they find a plant with aphids the hoverflies lay their eggs amongst the leaves, which hatch into larvae with an almost insatiable appetite for aphids, thus providing natural pest control right where it's most needed. French marigolds are thought to keep whitefly and aphids away from greenhouse tomatoes. Some say that this is because their pungent scent acts as a deterrent or disguises the presence of other crops from the pests. Not everyone believes this, but it works for me – even if it didn't, the fragrance of this colourful annual is well worth the effort of sowing them.

WEED CONTROL

Most weeds cannot be eradicated overnight, so often a slower, greener approach is a better way to deal with them. When I worked in a large garden, rather than spray borders that were riddled with couch grass and bindweed with weedkiller, the old head gardener would have me dig up the perennial herbaceous plants in early spring. I'd then pull out all the fleshy weed roots from the roots and soil around these herbaceous plants and replant them in a spare patch of ground to reuse later in the year. The border was then deeply forked through to remove the rest of the weed roots, and pretty cottage-garden annuals sown to fill up the spaces. In the autumn, when the annual bedding plants had died down, the border was clear of weeds and ready for the original perennial herbaceous plants to be moved back into.

FILL UP DIFFICULT PLACES

Plants that have grown from seed sown directly into the soil are more likely to survive than if they have been planted out as adults. This is because their growth is naturally tailored to suit their surroundings, as they grow up tough and are more self-reliant. Once they arc established, most seed-sown plants can 'self-sow' without you having to lift a finger. In this way, annuals will spread themselves around the garden to fill difficult areas with beautiful flowers. Californian poppies are ideal for this in dry shallow soils, while Busy Lizzies, and biennials such as honesty and foxgloves will all make their home in semi-shade.

GUILT-FREE CUT FLOWERS

Summer is all about abundance, and annuals certainly provide that. Most of them bear so many blooms that there are always enough to cut for the house. If you want a serious amount of flowers for cutting, set aside a separate border, around 120 x 120cm (4 x 4ft), or a corner on the allotment, and sow annual flower seeds in rows for picking. Pick regularly to keep them flowering for longer. Many annuals flower from June until the first frosts, but you can extend the season by planting daffodil and tulip bulbs in autumn for cut flowers throughout the spring.

PROPAGATING YOUR OWN PLANTS FROM CUTTINGS AND DIVISIONS

Once you start taking cuttings it becomes part of the rhythm of the year. It might seem like deferred gratification, but if you make this most rewarding of activities part of your calendar there will always be something coming to fruition. Unlike sowing, which introduces genetic variations, taking cuttings and dividing your plants creates exact replicas, so it is ideal for increasing the numbers of unusual or particularly good growers, petal colours or shapes.

HARDWOOD CUTTINGS

This is the simplest way to propagate trees and woody shrubs. It is so easy that even branches blown off the tree by wind can re-root and grow if they come into contact with the soil. Our prehistoric ancestors noticed how trees were able to do this and began pushing twigs of unusual or useful plants into the soil where they lived to mark their territories. It is still the best way to grow your own hedge – lengthy, wildlife-friendly boundaries of beech, hawthorn, sloe and crab apples. Hardwood cuttings also come into their own for fruit – gooseberries, loganberries, and blackcurrants will easily grow and be large enough to crop after a few summers.

Take hardwood cuttings when branches are bare in autumn and winter. Use secateurs to take pencil-thick stems from the last summer's growth (easily visible by their paler colour) and trim them to 20cm (8in) below a bud at the thicker, bottom end and to just above a bud at the top. If you are taking lots of cuttings it pays to prepare them all at once and to slant the cuts at the tops so it's easy to see that they are the right way up. Some gardeners say this slant also allows rot-causing moisture to drain away, but I've never found it makes a difference.

To strike the cuttings, make a slit in the soil with a spade and push the cuttings down into it, spacing them a hands-width apart. I was taught that the recommended depth in the soil is four-fifths of their length, leaving 5cm (2in) above the ground. This ensures that there are a good number of below-ground buds to turn into roots and a cluster above the soil to form a thicket of branches.

The cutting will naturally develop a shrubby, multi-stemmed shape that is fine for some bushes, but not ideal for many trees that are better as lollipops with a clear trunk and all the branches at the top. To get a tree-shaped cutting off to the best start, I've found it pays to push the cutting into the ground so that only the very top bud protrudes above the soil. This directs all the plants oomph into this bud and gives you a long, single shoot as opposed to a cluster of shorter ones.

After one summer of growth, carefully dig up the cutting, with the roots and surrounding soil, and either pot it up or plant it out where it is to grow. Take care to keep it well watered in dry periods.

SOFTWOOD AND SEMI-RIPE CUTTINGS

Use this technique for propagating flowers and flowering shrubs. Softwood cuttings are taken in May and June, while stems are filled with water and are soft, whereas semi-ripe cuttings are taken in midsummer-autumn, just as the current season's shoots start to harden. Softwood cuttings, from plants such as tomatoes and petunias, catch up with the parents and will even flower the same summer, while semi-ripes, after a winter in a coldframe, are large enough for planting out in their second summer.

You can always tell the right consistency for a semi-ripe cutting when you bend the stem. If it snaps it is either under

Taking semi-ripe *osteospermum* cuttings

or overripe, so you are looking for bendy, pliable shoots without flowers. Semi-ripe cuttings are great for lavenders, osteospermum, wallflowers, pelargoniums, penstemon, argyranthemums and woody herbs, such as rosemary and thyme. It serves the double purpose of propagating new plants and having back-ups in case parent plants are killed by a cold winter. Softwood cuttings are good for bulking up your bedding plants.

The simplest way to take both softwood and semi-ripe cuttings is to take a piece of the parent plant and pop it in a vase of water. After a few weeks, when a white tassel of roots starts to grow, pot them up into very wet compost to wean them off their aquatic life, then grow them on in the normal way. For more stocky plants, quickly snip a non-flowering shoot from the plant about 10cm (4in) long and remove the bottom half of the stem. Trim the stem with a sharp knife just below a bud (previous page, 1) and then use the knife to remove any snags from the cut or removed leaves, as these tend to rot on contact with compost.

Rooting hormone, which also contains a fungicide to reduce the risk of rotting, is one of those things you are either wedded to or not. I only use it if I'm taking a cutting of something I don't want to take chances with, or hard-to-come-by cuttings. Just dip the end of the cutting in the powder then push the stems into the pot of compost (2) – don't use a dibber if you don't have to as the action of pushing down through the gritty cuttings compost scrapes the outer layer and triggers growth cells to produce roots, thereby encouraging faster rooting. For softwood you will have to use a dibber.

Make sure the leaves sit just above the compost, water in and cover the whole pot with a clear plastic bag to hold moisture round the top (3). The key now is to keep the roots warm and the shoots cool, so keep newly taken cuttings out of full sun. Check them regularly to air the cuttings and remove any that show signs of rot. When new growth appears from the leaf axils, take off the plastic bag. Pot on cuttings individually into 9cm ($3^1/_2$in) pots once the roots come through the holes in the base. Keep plants grown from semi-ripe cuttings in a greenhouse/coldframe for planting out after the frosts the following year. Use plants from softwood cuttings in patio pots or plant out into the garden after frosts.

tip
Don't cover grey- or hairy-leaved cuttings with plastic as condensation sticks to the leaves and may introduce rots.

ROOT CUTTINGS

All herbaceous plants with carrot-like tap roots, such as verbascum, *Crambe cordifolia*, comfrey and sea hollies, can be propagated by slicing pieces of root from the parent and potting them up. If you want lots of plants, dig up the whole plant in the winter and set about chopping the roots into 10cm (4in) sections. Otherwise, leave the parent plant in the soil and scrape a few roots from the ground, but make sure you give the parent a good water afterwards to help it recover.

Roots that naturally grow straight down into the soil can be buried in the same way, on their ends, straight into the potting compost. Make sure they go into the compost the right way up (it's easy to get confused, but the thinner end goes down) and plant three to four per 10cm (4in) pot so they quickly bulk up into useable clumps.

Many herbaceous plants with more spreading roots will also grow from root cuttings, such as catmint, phlox, primula, oriental poppies, bleeding heart, and Japanese anemones. These can simply be cut to 10cm (4in) lengths, then laid flat and just buried in 10cm (4in) pots of compost. Fresh leaves will sprout along the length of the cuttings.

Leave root cuttings in pots and keep them in a coldframe to grow on and catch up with the parent plant. If you sit them in a heated propagator (see p.183) to first start growing and move to a coldframe, they'll be large enough to plant out in autumn of the following year.

DIVISIONS

Most perennial herbaceous plants are vigorous and grow on spreading roots that tend to roam away from where you planted them in search of fresh nutrients, leaving bare, dead patches in place of the original plants. Digging up and dividing their roots, when the plants are dormant (spring for some, autumn for others), serves two purposes. Firstly it makes new plants and regenerates old ones, and secondly it is a handy way to get free plants from friends or to take some of your favourites with you when you move house.

Autumn is the time when most herbaceous perennials are divided, when they first go to ground. Some are so vigorous, however, that you can practically chop them back at any time of year and they will recover and grow. Those that are a little more precious will die if they are not divided in the spring when they are actively growing. As a rule, these precious plants tend to be the ones that flower late in the season, such as *Echinacea*, Michaelmas daisies, ornamental grasses and *Helenium*. They come into growth when the temperatures start to rise and, if chopped about and sat back into cold soils, tend to rot away.

Dig the plant up from the ground with a spade and have a look at the roots. If they are fibrous, put two back-to-back forks into the centre of the plant and lever the handles towards each other to split the roots apart. If the roots are fleshy, use a spade to chop up the clumps. The more divisions you make, the more plants you will get, but the smaller they will be and the longer they will take to bulk up. Ideally, aim for clumps that are just a bit larger than you buy in a pot – around 20cm (8in) across. Remove any dead and unproductive roots with secateurs while you are doing this.

COLLECTING SEED

The prime time to collect seed is in early autumn, although it's worth looking out for ripe seed from midsummer onwards. The seedheads are ready for harvest when they are dry and the seed readily tumbles from the spent blooms. Cut the whole heads into a paper bag on a dry day and put them somewhere to dry.

After a few weeks, when the seeds are completely dry, they can be winnowed. On a still day, crumble the seeds and cases into a bowl, go outside and gently toss them into the air while blowing across the airborne seeds. The seed, being heavier than the chaff, falls back into the bowl while the rest blows away.

Annuals, such as cosmos, tobacco plants and marigolds are easiest to grow from seed, but they won't come true (look exactly like the parent). The economy from collecting seed is really apparent when it comes to plants that look best in large groups, such as foxgloves, teasel and ox-eye daisies, and design styles that demand groups, such as prairie planting, ornamental grasses, knautia and *Verbena bonariensis*.

RIGHT: Fennel seed and opium poppy (below) are such prolific seed makers you might want to collect some and give them to friends!

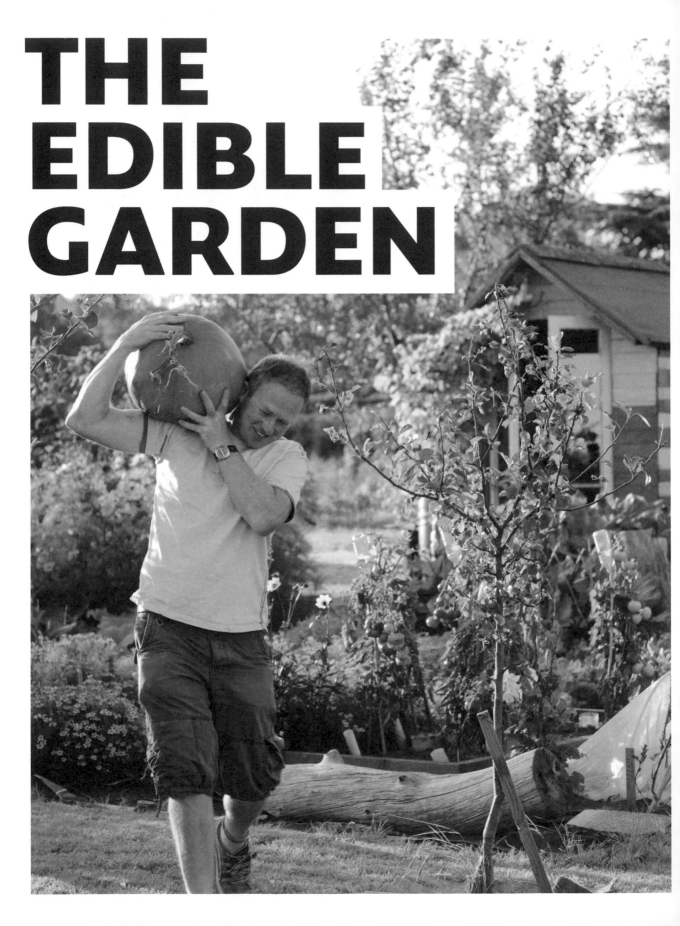

THE EDIBLE GARDEN

Growing your own fruit and vegetables can give you a wonderful feeling of wealth. People who have never enjoyed the particular sense of satisfaction you get from picking a bowlful of blueberries or peas may be bemused by what appears to be a lot of effort for small returns. But what they don't know is that just one less vegetable on your shopping list and one more home-grown carrot on your plate makes you feel more in touch with yourself and your needs. It gives you a deep sense of self-reliance, if not quite self-sufficiency. And yes, it's true, home-grown food really does taste far superior to anything you can buy. It's fresh, full of flavour, free of unknowns and packed with the sweet flavour of success.

STARTING A VEGETABLE GARDEN OR ALLOTMENT

Whether you grow vegetables in your garden or take on an allotment, a sunny spot and weed-free soil is essential. This doesn't just mean weeding before you sow, you have to get rid of the perennial weeds, such as bindweed, which will come up and strangle your crops. The basic rule of thumb is to dig deep, then you can pull them out to the depth of your fork. However, you won't be able to escape them entirely, so my advice to beginners is not to take on too big an area in one go.

Start out with a minimum size of 2 x 2m (6 x 6ft) and mulch over the rest of the space with a weed-suppressing membrane, such as an old carpet, for at least one season to starve the weeds of light. I've been growing vegetables for more than ten years, both in the garden and on allotments, and for minimum effort and maximum crops this is what I believe to be the best method.

A GARDEN OR AN ALLOTMENT?

If you've got the space and the right conditions, grow vegetables in your garden because it's handy and you will have easy access to water, which is not always guaranteed on allotments. If space is limited, use the garden for herbs and salad crops, and get an allotment for larger crops that need to stay in the soil for a long time, such as root crops like carrots, potatoes, parsnips and

perennial crops such as rhubarb and asparagus. If you have space I would also recommend a greenhouse, as it will give you early crops of herbs and salads and a guaranteed harvest of tender tomatoes and chilli peppers no matter how dreary and wet the summer is.

In a garden setting I think it looks neater and more attractive to grow vegetables in timber-edged beds where they can look formal or cottage-like, depending on whether you surround the beds with a picket fence or a grand yew hedge. For more information about how to build raised beds and ideas for designs, see p.42.

If you don't have much space or would rather reserve your garden for flower borders, take on an allotment. Before you go down this route, although have a think about how much time you want to spend there and how far away it is, and choose your crops accordingly. If you can only spend one day a week at the allotment then the best crops are low-maintenance plants such as fruit trees, perennial herbs and soft fruit, along with plants that can be left to their own devices, such as potatoes, cabbages, runner beans and parsnips. Alternatively, you could consider an allotment-share with a friend.

If you know you will be a frequent visitor to the allotment, your options are far greater – as will be the work! Check out if there is water on-site before you take it on, if there isn't you will need a shed and a water butt, but take care because some allotment committees don't allow permanent structures.

CROP ROTATION

Crop rotation is simply working to a plan so that different crops are grown in different parts of your plot every year. This reduces the likelihood of pests and disease building up and enables you to prepare and feed the soil for hungry crops and avoid wasting valuable horse manure and soil improver on vegetables that won't appreciate it.

The simplest system involves dividing crops into four groups: roots (such as parsnips, carrots, potatoes); brassicas (such as cabbages, kale); legumes (peas and beans); and 'others', which

LEFT TOP: Lifting potatoes in early June on the allotment.

LEFT BOTTOM: Late summer with a fleece cloche in the foreground to keep caterpillars off my young cabbages.

includes tomatoes, spinach and sweet corn. Divide your kitchen garden into four beds and rotate the crops between the beds each year. Although this system is good, allotments and kitchen gardens seldom divide into equally sized areas, let alone plots with equal light or soil quality. Also, unlike farmers, gardeners usually intensely grow a wider variety of plants, filling in spaces between rows and replacing crops twice, sometimes three times, a season. So, rather than sticking rigidly to a plan, I try to leave a two-year gap between visits to the same spot and keep track of what has grown where by taking pictures with a digital camera.

I still follow some rules, though. I always feed the soil with manure before planting hungry potatoes, compost before carrots (manure makes them fork) and follow legumes with brassicas. Legumes gather and store the plant food nitrogen on their roots, so if their roots are left in the soil the nitrogen will promote leafy growth on cabbages, and the un-dug, settled soil encourages them to heart up well.

tip

A plastic box is the best for storing seed. Keep it on a shelf, out of the sun, where it will stay dry and cool. Not all seed is worth keeping from season to season, though – carrot, swede and parsnip seeds, for example, don't store well and need to be bought fresh every year.

GUIDE TO POPULAR VEGETABLES

These are some of the most popular and easy to grow vegetables. For more information on seed sowing, see pp.98–102, advice on potting compost, p.89, sowing directly into the ground, p.108 and for growing crops in the greenhouse, see p.185. Good luck!

ARTICHOKE (GLOBE)

There are a few varieties of globe artichoke, but they all taste the same. They can be grown from seed, but results can be variable so only keep the most vigorous seedlings for growing on. More often plants are sold as 'slips' – leafy side-shoots with roots – that are sometimes potted up. Plant slips in a sunny position, in soil that drains well in the winter. In the first summer, trim off the thistle-like flowers (globes) early to encourage the roots and leaves to bulk up. In the second year, harvest the globes before the fluffy centre, or 'choke', is visible, leaving a 12cm (5in) stem attached to the globe. Other smaller globes can then grow

Tactile and tasty globe artichoke buds, just at the right stage for harvesting.

from the buds beneath the cut stem. Allow your artichoke to self-seed into a clump by leaving a few globes to drop their seeds.

Many gardeners grow artichokes, but few know how or bother to cook the plump, thistle-like flowers they produce. Separating the edible parts from the rest can be fiddly, so what I do is cook small (golf-ball-sized) heads whole, in oil, for a few minutes; or larger heads in boiling water for 45 minutes. Serve them whole and enjoy their creamy texture and nutty flavour.

ARTICHOKE (JERUSALEM)

Two things are always said about these crunchy, sweet tubers – they are effortless to grow and cause terrible wind! A chef once told me that their anti-social side can be reduced by replacing the water in which they are boiled a couple of times while they are cooking. On the easy to grow front, they can be left to their own devices and make colourful windbreaks on exposed plots, but they grow much bigger and the tubers are easier to peel if the plants are dug up every winter. Replant the smoothest and largest tubers 45cm (18in) apart in freshly composted soil in winter, and you will harvest much better-quality tubers.

'Fuseau' is the best variety as it is the most smooth skinned. Always plant Jerusalem artichokes in the sun, and if you've got a damp, heavy clay plant them on ridges, around 5cm (2in) above the soil, to improve drainage.

ASPARAGUS

Asparagus is one of the most worthwhile and rewarding crops you can grow. It requires a little patience as there is a seasons' wait between planting and the first picking, but from then on the crops just get bigger and better. Apart from weeding, asparagus demands little attention, and home-grown spears are so superior to anything you can buy you will soon wonder how you lived without it for so long!

They have quite fiddly planting requirements that involve planting the roots into a trench then gradually topping up the soil until it reaches the surrounding soil level. This technique allows the young shoots to quickly find the light and energy they need to grow as fast and vigorously as possible to guarantee plenty of spears by the third year, otherwise you would potentially have to wait even longer for the plants to bulk up.

All-male varieties, such as 'Grolim', have thicker spears than mixed sex types, such as the classic 'Connover's Colossal'. Purple varieties, such as 'Purple Pacific', are the most tender. Buy asparagus plants as bare roots, either from nurseries or by mail order, in the spring. Before you plant them, drop the spidery roots into a bucket of water to rehydrate them for an hour or so, by which time they will have plumped up. Then start digging out a 30cm- (1ft-) wide trench; 30cm (1ft) deep for thick spears, or 15cm (6in) deep for thin spears (the planting depth does make a difference), in full sun and well-drained soil. Weed the area thoroughly and fork plenty of compost into the trench now, because you won't be able to dig around the plants once they are planted. Run your spade along the base of the trench to create a ridge to sit the crowns on and then, spacing them 45cm (18in) apart, spread their roots over the trench and backfill to just cover them.

When shoots start to appear in spring, top up the soil level an inch or so at a time and keep them watered as the weather warms. Hand-weed religiously, but don't pick the shoots in the first year to allow the plant to build up strength. In the second summer you can take a few spears from each crown, slicing them off with a sharp knife just below soil level when they are 18cm (7in) tall. In the third year, cut the shoots in earnest, but stop harvesting after six weeks and allow the shoots to grow to help

the plants recover for the following year. On windy sites, stake the frond-like foliage with twigs. In the autumn, cut off any berry-bearing fronds so they don't self-sow.

LEFT: Harvest asparagus spears just below the soil surface

RIGHT: 'Cylindra' types of beetroot give you more slices per root than the globes.

AUBERGINES

For reliable crops aubergines need to be grown in a greenhouse (see p.185). If you don't have a greenhouse, buy ready-grown plants in late April or May. Harden off plants and grow in well-composted soil in the sunniest spot you have got and keep your fingers crossed for a good summer – if it's hot and the summer goes on into September, you will get a harvest; two or three fruits per plant. Feed with a tomato fertilizer as soon as fruits appear.

BEETROOT

Beetroot has had a renaissance; it is not just about pickling and stained hands any more, beetroot is also great for making succulent cakes, crisps and of course baby leaves. I wrap my beetroot in tinfoil and pop it in with the Sunday roast to mush into the gravy, and I always sow a few early plants for picking as zesty, fresh cut-and-come-again leaves.

Whether you sow in the greenhouse in pots or directly into sunny borders, depends on what you want and when.

tip

When you thin out your beetroot seedlings, don't throw the leaves away – use the thinnings as tasty salad leaves.

PLAYING CATCH-UP

If you miss the window for sowing, don't despair – these tricks will help you cheat the season. They are also useful in colder gardens where the summer season is short:

■ Sow in pots inside on the windowsill. This can knock two weeks off cropping times for beans, and works well for all vegetables, except root crops that tend to 'fork' if they are grown in short containers.

■ 'Tent' late-planted crops with open-ended cloches. I use 40cm (16in) squares of toughened glass on my allotment. This works as a shortcut for hardening off the plants, and provides enough extra heat to encourage growth without cooking them.

■ Sprout seed by wrapping it in moist kitchen paper and putting it in a sealed jar in the airing cupboard. It will then sprout in days, rather than weeks, and can be potted up as soon as the radicle (the first root) pokes through the seed coat. This works best for larger seeds such as pumpkins and courgettes – I've had crops of both from a late-July sowing!

■ Cover the soil with black plastic for a week (ideally two) before planting. This warms the soil in early spring, and for late-planted crops the plastic keeps the soil moist by catching condensation.

■ Increase light levels with light-coloured, crushed shell mulches that bounce extra light up onto the plants. Shell mulches and white plastic sheeting works well in greenhouses too.

■ Use cloches to protect late-sown, low-growing plants in autumn, and fleece for taller tender vegetables such as runner beans. This will keep them productive beyond the first frost, which is often followed by a period of clement weather.

■ Beach-style windbreaks are brilliant for protecting early-planted tender-vegetables, such as sweet corn, from cold winds. Form a corral that is open ended to the south to trap warm air and protect the plants from cold northerly blasts.

In early spring, sow bolt-resistant varieties, such as 'Boltardy', which copes with heat and dry summer weather without bolting to flower. For autumn and winter crops, sow main-crop varieties in early summer. For baby leaves, sow seeds in-easy-to-reach blocks in semi-shade, but if you are growing beetroot for the roots, sow the plants in full sun. Apart from for baby leaves, sow seeds 1cm (½in) deep in well-watered drills (scrapes in the soil). Once the green shoots appear, thin them out so they are spaced roughly 5cm (2in) apart for baby roots, 10cm (4in) apart for summer globes, and 15cm (6in) for winter crops. Keep the plants watered and weed-free, and harvest from when they are the size of a ping-pong ball (depending on the variety) by lifting alternate beets to allow the ones left behind to grow larger in the cleared space.

BROAD BEANS

I love broad beans. They are ready for picking in late spring; either whole like runner beans when they are just a couple of inches long, or as beans once they have filled out their quilted pods and you can see the shape of the beans under the skin.

Sow them in sandy, free-draining soil in the autumn, but if your beds are wet and sticky, wait until spring. The plants will be up and bearing pods by the end of May (if sown in the autumn) through to June (if sown in the spring) and will be over just in time to plant a follow-on crop of pumpkins or sweet corn in their place. It also means you will get a crop before the dreaded black bean aphids attack. Push the beans knuckle-deep, straight into good garden soil in a sunny position, spacing them 20cm (8in) apart. I plant mine in double rows, with a gap between them that is just wide enough for me to get down for picking. Once the plants are about 30cm (1ft) high, they need support or they will flop, so I push two 1m (40in) stakes 30cm (1ft) apart at either end of the row and corral them with a loop of string tied around the canes.

Broad beans are particularly prone to blackfly. Keep an eye out for aphids and snap off the leafy tips to help keep the number down and also encourage the beans to swell. If you see notches at

Twist broad beans from the plant with one hand, holding the stem, which can easily snap, with the other.

the edges of leaves, you may have bean weevil. The plants will often outgrow this pest unless they are still young plants, in which case use an organic contact insecticide and hoe around the plants to expose the larvae and overwintering beetles to the birds. Rotate your crop the following year to avoid reinfestation.

BRASSICAS

Brassicas are all members of the cabbage family. They have been bred from the wild cabbage to produce either large flowers, like cauliflowers; lots of buds, like sprouts; or single large buds, like cabbages. They all like similar soils, so I have only mentioned the basic growing information in cabbages, to save repetition.

■ Cabbages

The various different cabbages, whether red, autumn, summer or winter cabbages, may have different sowing times, but share a preference for firm ground (to heart up) and alkaline soils. So if you have to prepare the ground in advance of sowing, leave the soil to settle for a few weeks before planting, especially if it is a light, sandy or chalky soil. Add lime in the autumn if the pH of your soil is below 6.5.

Red cabbages are the tastiest and best-looking cabbage: they are tangy and delicious when cooked or soaked in a marinade made from apple or orange juice. The reds are late-summer and autumn croppers and will often hang on in a mild spot until Christmas. My favourite winter variety is Savoy – they are not as tough tasting as the green types, and their crinkled leaves hold on to gravy and sauces much better.

All cabbages have a long list of pests, from aphids and flea-beetle to whitefly and caterpillars, so I always cover young plants under a blanket of horticultural fleece to keep them at bay. If the fleece won't stay in place – it can be a challenge as larger autumn and winter croppers fill out – change tactics. Be on the lookout for clusters of tiny round yellow eggs that cluster on the underside of leaves and stems, and squash them before they turn into caterpillars. Also, take off any yellow leaves as they harbour aphids. Your plants may start to look ragged, but if you can keep them limping along until September, they will put on a growth spurt and recover as the frosts kill the

tip

When harvesting cabbages, slice off the tops and score an 'x' in the stump to encourage an extra crop of greens to re-grow.

leaf-eating bugs. Club-root, as the name suggests, causes swollen roots and kills all brassicas. It can be a serious problem on allotments, so help prevent it by rotating your crops every season. If it is a problem on your site, burn the affected plants and start cabbages off in pots, planting them out when large to reduce the chances of infection.

Sow summer cabbages, little-and-often, in situ from late winter to late spring for a constant supply through summer. Thin to adjust the spacing from 20cm (8in) up to 40cm (16in) to create a mix of large and dinner-sized heads. For the largest heads, water the plants really well two weeks before picking.

Sow autumn and winter cabbages in cell trays or a seedbed (a spare weed-free patch). Move them to their proper planting positions when other crops vacate them. Growing them in seedbeds is better, as their roots are inevitably torn during the replanting process and the plants respond by re-growing a more fibrous root system so they grow into bushier plants. Plant so that the lower leaves are just above the soil surface in sunshine.

■ Brussels sprouts

Grow these like winter cabbages, but stake them in late summer by tying their stems to bamboo canes as they grow. Pile about 10cm (2in) of soil around the stems to anchor their roots in the

LEFT: Keep weeds at bay by hoeing between rows of plants.

RIGHT: Brassicas sown in May are ready to plant out by the summer.

Remove tatty pest-harbouring leaves from Brussels sprouts.

RIGHT: Tuscan kale is perennial and can be left on the plot for a few years for winter pickings.

autumn, and remove all yellow leaves as they appear. Harvest the sprouts from the bottom of the plant up when they are about the size of a conker. The leaves that grow on top of the plant make tasty winter greens too.

■ Calabrese

This worthwhile summer crop is best sown like spring cabbage, at intervals, for a succession of pickings. For really big heads – I've grown them 35cm (14in) wide – water the plants well when the flower heads appear. Harvest them by slicing off the heads with a stalk about a hands-width long. If you liquid-feed with a general balanced plant fertilizer and water the plant well, smaller calabreselettes will develop from the side shoots.

■ Cauliflowers

This is the fussiest of the brassicas. It needs good soil and a fleece is essential otherwise aphids will take up residence within the white flowers (known as curds). Mulch the plants, and keep the soil moist as they grow. As they start to mature, fold the leaves around the curds to keep the sun off them in summer and to protect them from frosts in winter. Space plants around 60–65cm (2ft) apart for the largest curds, but unless you are running a restaurant, half that distance will be big enough for a family feeding of cauliflower cheese. Always pick when the florets are still tight because they quickly deteriorate once the flowers start to open. So if it looks ready, it is!

■ Kale

Kale grows best on a limy soil, but it is less fussy or prone to common cabbage diseases than other brassicas. Sow seeds in trays in the greenhouse or coldframe in April and transplant them individually into 8cm (3in) pots and put them outside 45cm (18in) apart. Alternatively, sow seeds directly and thin out the seedlings. Wash aphids from the leaves with a hose and pick off any yellowing leaves that might be harbouring pests. If your site is windy, anchor the plants by drawing up about 5cm (2in) of soil around the base of each plant. Harvest the leaves after the cold weather arrives in late autumn, picking the tasty young leaves and leaving the crowns to re-sprout for follow-on pickings through until March.

■ Winter sprouting broccoli

Sow and grow winter sprouting broccoli like winter cabbages. Purple types are the most reliable, the white is less so but has a more delicate flavour. Harvest the numerous flowerbuds little and often from late winter through to early spring.

SWEDES

Swedes are a wonderful home-grown root crop, and are much crunchier than the slow-to-cook cannon balls which are available in the shops. I sow them in cell trays in the early summer (they come up more reliably than if they are sown directly), and then plant them out, under fleece, when they are small. The roots are ready to harvest in the early winter. Grow in sun, and in any soil except acidic.

CARROTS

Carrots are best sown directly into the soil any time from February to August. Match the variety of carrot to the sowing time: 'Early' and 'short-rooted' varieties produce fast crops from late winter/spring sowings and again from late-summer

BOOMERANG VEGETABLES

Some vegetables are one-season wonders that need to be re-sown every spring, while others keep cropping for years. This ability to 'boomerang' back into production, with little effort on your part, makes them must-have plants:

■ **Globe and Jerusalem artichokes.** Statuesque plants for summer and winter crops.

■ **Asparagus.** A plant I'd never be without, there's nothing to beat its fresh-picked flavour.

■ **Rhubarb.** A classic, sun-loving plant.

■ **Schorzonera.** An unusual parsnip-like root-crop.

■ **Sprouting broccoli.** Not often done, but one plant on my plot cropped through four winters and turned into a dome-shaped shrub.

■ **Sea kale.** A hardy native perennial of Britain's seashores.

■ **Japanese spring onions.** Ishikuro is a Welsh onion relative that will turn into a chive-like clump.

■ **Self-seeders.** These include orach, grain amaranth and salsify.

sowings; larger maincrop varieties need to be sown during spring/early summer. Maincrops don't develop their flavour until autumn, but being large, they hold on to moisture well and keep right through the winter. The earlies are less substantial, but super-sweet and delicious from bite-size upwards.

Ideally carrots like sunny, stone-free soil with lots of compost and leaf mould dug in the previous winter, otherwise they will 'fork'. If you have forgotten or don't have time to do this, and your soil is heavy, make a slit in the soil with your spade and fill it with sand. Alternatively, if your soil is stony, try growing early carrots ('Early Nantes' is good) in raised beds or pots.

Once the seedlings come up, thin them out to 10cm (4in) apart to get good-sized carrots. Hand weed along the rows and watch out for slugs. Carrots are especially prone to carrot root fly – a grub that burrows through the roots. Keep plants covered with a layer of horticultural fleece to protect them from this pest, and only thin seedlings on dull overcast evenings when fewer carrot flies are about. Drawing soil up over the crowns also makes it harder for carrot fly to find the roots, and blanches the otherwise sour-tasting green tops to make them sweet. Start harvesting from early summer and either leave maincrop carrots in the ground for winter, or if your soil is heavy or there is a bad winter, lift the roots and store them in boxes of moist sand.

tip

Cover seed with leaf mould or spent potting compost, as this will help hold moisture around the seed and make germination less erratic.

CELERIAC

Celeriac might be a vegetable ugly duckling, but compared to celery it is a breeze to grow and delicious chipped or mashed. I start the seed off in 5cm (2in) cells and plant the seedlings out in a sunny spot in ordinary garden soil when the roots show through the drainage holes. Celery leaf miner – an insect that bores between the layers of the leaves creating a marbled effect on them – can be a problem, so keep on top of it by nipping off affected leaves. On allotments, where this pest can be prolific, keep the plants covered with fleece until they are established.

Harvest celeriac from early autumn through to Christmas, and beyond if the weather is mild. The tangy leaves are great when added to soups.

RIDGE CUCUMBERS AND GHERKINS

If you want to grow cucumbers outdoors, the types to go for are the ridge cucumbers and gherkins, such as 'American Pickling', which is always a winner. I've never pickled it, but when eaten fresh they are small and ideal for a single meal. The name 'ridge' comes from the technique of planting them on 30cm (12in) mounds of soil – a technique that is good if your garden is poorly drained. I plant them like courgettes – in rich, manure-improved soil with plenty of sun and space – and leave them to trail over a

LEFT: 'Chantenay' carrots – the best early carrots for clay soils.

RIGHT: Gherkins are like cucumbers but with a more tangy taste. You can eat them fresh, there's no need to pickle them.

mulch of straw. Compared to greenhouse cucumbers the flavour of outdoor types is more intense, although the thicker skins make peeling essential.

Sow the seeds indoors on a windowsill or in a greenhouse in late March or April, singly and on their sides in 8cm (3in) pots. Put them in a propagator set to 21°C (70°F) and plant them out in May, after the frost and when they have three good leaves, in borders or 30cm (12in) tubs on the patio. Keep well watered in dry weather.

FLORENCE FENNEL

These tangy aniseed bulbs are delicious roasted or finely sliced and tossed into a vinaigrette and are one of my favourite late-summer crops. Sow them direct after the longest day in the summer – any earlier and the plants will flower, making the bulbs fibrous and tough. Allow 35cm (14in) between rows and a similar distance between each plant – thin them out as and when the leaves crowd together. Always thin the plants by pulling them up roots-and-all, but once they have their 35cm (14in) spacing, use a knife to slice the bulbs from the roots. If you cut just above the bottom leaves, two smaller bulbs will re-sprout. Although the frost may damage the foliage, the fennel bulbs will stay good up until Christmas.

LEEKS

The 'mid-season' leeks that crop in winter are the ones I like the best – I love their warming sweet flavour in hearty soups and casseroles – although early and late types are also available, cropping in autumn and spring respectively. I start the seeds off in cell trays, and when the leaves are about 20cm (8in) tall, plant them 15cm (6in) apart with 30cm (1ft) between the rows.

Large leeks should always be sown in one place – a seed bed or cell tray – and moved to another so that they can be planted deep. Trowel out 15cm (6in) holes for each one and drop the plants into the bottom, so that their stems, but not the lower part of their leaves, sit beneath the soil level. Do not back-fill and firm around the plants in the normal way, just drop the plants into the hole and water them in using a watering can with a rose attachment to wash a little soil over the roots as you go. Over time the holes will fill up with soil and cover the stems,

tip

Don't worry if your leek plants lean to one side, they will naturally straighten up on their own.

which will turn white in the darkness and develop a sweeter flavour than the green tops. When you are transplanting, don't bother with the old practice of trimming the leaves and roots – it won't improve the eventual size of the leeks – only plenty of compost dug into good rich soil will do that.

Huge, prize-winning leeks are hard to grow, but crops of sweet baby leeks are quite easy to produce by sowing seeds 5cm (2in) apart in rows through spring and summer. They may be smaller, but they crop more quickly and make an easy onion alternative that is just as delicious.

Leeks are generally fairly undemanding, but look out for rust – a fungal disease that shows up as orange blobs on the leaves, often in wet, humid years. To combat this, avoid high-nitrogen feeds and smear petroleum jelly on the blobs to prevent further spread. As with all vegetables, rotate your crops and grow them in a different spot each year to prevent fungal spores building up in the soil.

MARROW, SQUASH, PUMPKIN AND COURGETTE

About as similar in appearance as Arnold Schwarzenegger and Danny De Vito, courgettes, marrows and pumpkins are all members of the same sun-loving family and, for me, summer wouldn't be the same without them.

LEFT: Some Florence fennel are tall and thin, others wide and fat, but all add a delicious aniseed twist to salads and roasts.

RIGHT: Super-reliable courgette 'Defender' has never failed to give me a crop.

GROWING A MONSTER

Never mind the flavour, here's how to grow a giant:

■ Use seed of large varieties. 'Atlantic Giant' is the most commonly sold type, but even better seeds can be bought from specialist show-vegetable suppliers.

■ Start plants off in a greenhouse or inside and harden them off before planting outside.

■ Enrich the soil with a barrow load of well-rotted manure, forked into the soil.

■ Warm the improved soil under black plastic for about two weeks before planting.

■ Mulch the plants with compost after planting out.

■ Water the plants well as the weather heats up in summer.

■ Pinch off fruit and flowers until the plant reaches 2–3m (6–10ft), then allow one fruit to develop.

■ As the pumpkin grows, lift and support it on a bed of straw or old carpet to keep it from touching the soil. If it starts getting really large, rest it on a wooden pallet to make the final transport by truck to a weighbridge easier.

■ Adjust the position of the pumpkin so that the stem feeding it doesn't twist or become strained as the fruit swells.

■ Keep the plant growing by protecting it with fleece during cold spells in the early autumn.

■ Feed with a liquid seaweed feed once a week and a balanced fertilizer, or try to weasel a secret recipe from a seasoned giant-vegetable grower.

I love using courgettes in stir fries and cakes, the best (in my view) are the thin-skinned yellow types, although they only do well in hot summers, while summer squash are particularly delicious stuffed. The more unusual 'spaghetti' squash is famed for its noodle-like consistency, which, when cooked, soaks up tomato sauce like succulent pasta. Courgettes, marrows and spaghetti squash are ideal for summer eating, as even those like marrows (with thicker skins), will only keep for a few weeks. Pumpkins, or winter squash as they are also known, have thick rinds and will keep for months.

Not all pumpkins have the same flavour. Moschata has vermicelli flesh, hubbards are heartier, kabotchas are like sweet potato and delicata types are nutty. But all squashes like the same growing conditions. Sow them in late spring in the greenhouse or coldframe, but don't be tempted to sow any earlier otherwise they turn into triffids, hog all your greenhouse space and promote fungal diseases.

tip

Remove the first courgette a plant produces, as it seldom develops into a fruit worth eating and slows production of follow-on fruits.

Plant them out in late May/June and keep them well watered and fed with liquid feeds, such as a seaweed tonic, as soon as they start cropping. Watch out for slugs as they can destroy a young plant in a night. Pick courgettes as the flowers fall away or leave them to swell into marrows, but be aware that courgette production slows down and stops if they are not picked regularly. Remove leaves around pumpkins and squash to allow the flesh to ripen, and support the fruit with straw to keep the flesh clean and dry.

tip
Pinch off the first courgette, pepper and aubergine that form. This fruit tends to be quite tough and seedy so stopping it developing encourages more tender fruits to follow.

ONIONS

Onions are at the heart of almost every meal I make, so they get plenty of room on my allotment. Some gardeners grow them from seed, started off in winter and raised in cells inside, but I prefer the easier option of growing from heat-treated sets – small onion bulbs that have been heated to kill the embryonic flower in the centre, which means they won't run to flower (something that untreated sets are prone to do). If they are planted in late spring, in full sun with their noses just above the soil level, they swell into onions by late summer. Birds will often pull newly planted sets out of the ground, so cover them with mesh or trigs until the leaves start to grow.

To store onions, lift them carefully with a fork when the foliage has withered and fallen over, then dry them thoroughly in a greenhouse or under cloches before bagging up or tying onto strings (see p.141). They will keep until the following year. For an earlier summer crop, plant 'over-wintering' sets in the autumn. These are hardy, but must have good drainage around the roots or they will rot during winter. Their high water content means they only keep for a maximum of a few months after harvest as they're prone to rot, but they are ready from June.

All onions need sun and good soil, but avoid planting in recently manured ground as this will cause excessive lush growth at the expense of the bulbs. A five-month gap between digging in manure and planting onions is fine. Plant them in double rows, spaced 15cm (6in) apart, and hand weed between them rather than hoeing, which can damage the roots, causing rot or the plants to bolt. Crop rotation is also key, as there are many soil-borne pests and fungal diseases that are worse in wet years. Find a good open spot and rake up heavy soil before planting to improve the drainage.

MAKE AN ONION OR SHALLOT STRING

Although onions and shallots will keep in boxes or bags, the best way to store them is strung up, which allows air to circulate around them and prevents them from rotting. It is also far more convenient, as it allows you easy access to select large or small onions to suit whatever you are cooking.

Use rope or any thick string that will take the weight of the onions. Tie a loop in one end and hang the string above a door or anywhere it can hang freely. Tie another loop at the bottom end and begin to wind some onions, by their stalks, through the loop to create a 'pendulum' of onions at the bottom. Add more onions by wrapping their stalks around the string and sliding them down onto the 'pendulum' below. Continue until the string is full up then hang the finished string of onions in a cool frost-free shed, where they will keep until next summer.

SHALLOTS

There are several different types of shallot, but I like the reds for their strong flavour and the long French types as they are sweet and easy to slice. Plant shallots as sets from early winter to early spring, the date depends on how cold your garden is, but if the ground is workable (i.e. not frozen or wringing wet) get them in as soon as possible. The soil needs to be well dug, but settled as they don't do well in either compacted or fluffy soil. Space them 18cm (7in) apart – they need a little more room than onions as shallot bulbs split into clumps. Lift and store in the same way as onions, from midsummer.

LEFT: On my plot birds pull newly planted shallots from the ground so now I start them off in compost-filled trays indoors. After a fortnight roots develop which, when planted, anchor the bulbs in the soil.

SPRING ONIONS

Sow spring onions every few weeks from spring through until late summer in neutral or alkaline soil for a long succession of pickings. Japanese types – you can spot them by their names, such as 'Ishikura' – are well worth growing as, although they don't form bulbs, their stems are long, sweetly flavoured and will stay fresh in the ground for a long time before harvesting. Pull the crop when they are the thickness of a pencil and larger.

GARLIC

Garlic is very hardy and can, as the old adage goes, be planted on the shortest day and harvested on the longest. In truth, it can be planted from autumn onwards; the longer the growing season the bigger the bulbs.

Garlic can be bought as virus-free bulbs that you break up into cloves and plant individually – only plant the plumpest cloves as they grow into the biggest bulbs. Sun and a free-draining soil are all garlic needs, along with roughly a 15cm (6in) space between plants. When planting, the depth of the hole depends on the soil. In light, free-draining beds, make the hole about 10cm (4in) deep, but where the soil is heavy, make the hole half that depth. Drop the clove in the bottom and back-fill the soil. Never just push the cloves into the soil, as this can damage the root plate on the base. Hand weed and harvest

LEFT: Drying garlic ready for storing under a handmade glass cloche outdoors – the same trick works for onions.

MIDDLE AND RIGHT: 'Kelvedon Wonder' peas – the more you pick the more you get.

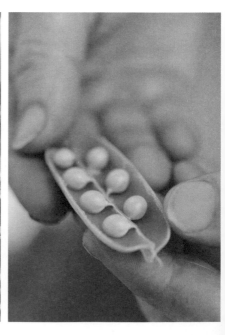

garlic in the same way as you would onions. Some varieties are prone to bolting, so if you notice bulbs running to flower, snap off the stems. Bulbs will still form, but they won't keep for more than a few weeks before deteriorating.

ORIENTAL GREENS, CHINESE CABBAGE AND PAK CHOI

These juicy, often spicy, orientals are super vegetables for sowing after the mid-summer point (they tend to bolt if they are sown earlier) in gaps that have been left after other crops have been harvested. They relish the heat of summer and, given plenty of water, will be ready for cropping within weeks. Scatter the seed on an empty bed, or sow it neatly in blocks or rows. Blocks are the best in raised beds where they will give the biggest yield in a small space. All types of orientals make good polytunnel crops, with mustards and mizunas proving pickings right through the winter. But beware, slugs and snails love oriental vegetables and will feast on the fast growth, as will leaf-holing flea beetles, so set slug traps and cover the plants with fleece to keep beetles at bay.

PARSNIPS

If you have an open, sunny spot with stone-free soil it is worth considering growing parsnips. All you need to do is weed the spring-sown seedlings once or twice as they grow and you will have a whole winter's-worth of delicious tangy roots to enjoy. 'Gladiator' and 'Tender and True' are very reliable, though be patient as parsnips are slow to germinate and can take up to 4 weeks to sprout. It is always worth buying new seed annually as it doesn't keep well, so for that reason it is worth sowing generously in rows 30cm (1ft) apart, gradually thinning the plants to leave 20cm (8in) between them. Don't manure the soil where you plan to sow as parsnips, like carrots, will fork if they are overfed. They will also fork if the roots are disturbed, so it is best to weed by hand rather than hoe. Wait until after the first frost to harvest, as this is when they will have the best flavour.

PEAS

Andi Clevely, a gardener and friend of mine, told me that when he worked in service in a grand house the cook always demanded

'Kelvedon Wonder' peas, as 'they taste the best'. After giving them a try I'd have to say that 'cook' was right – they are sweet, fill out their pods well and best of all are early croppers.

'Early' peas, as opposed to maincrops, are my favourite peas to grow. I start my first sowing in late winter, in compost-filled gutters in the greenhouse, and slide them out into the soil as a ready-grown row in early spring. I follow this up with a succession of sowings, directly into well-composted soil about 5cm (2in) apart, throughout the spring. A fleece cover will keep off foraging mice and birds until the plants are up and growing. Once the fleece is off, stake the plants with 1.2m (4ft) twigs. Harvest the swollen pods from midsummer onwards, and continue picking to keep the crop coming. When the crop is over, clear the spent stems, but leave the nitrogen-fixing roots in the ground to feed the next crop.

POTATOES

Potatoes come in different types: earlies, or new potatoes, for summer eating; second earlies for late summer/autumn; and maincrops for storing through winter. All love a rich soil improved with manure the previous autumn, and sun.

Buy potatoes as seed spuds in the winter to chit and plant in March/April. In recent years, wet weather has meant that

LEFT: Rub all but three sprouts off each of your 'chitted' potatoes. Instead of lots of small spuds you'll get half a dozen big 'uns.

RIGHT: Planting earlies in March.

LEARN TO SPEAK 'SPUD'

Although they are easy to grow, spuds have their own language that can be confusing, so here is a list of key terms:

■ **'Seed potatoes'.** These are baby potatoes that are ready for planting.

■ **'Certified virus free'.** This means the seed potatoes are in rude health, and free of diseases that could otherwise affect growth.

■ **'Chitting'.** The process of leaving the seed potatoes, on end, in a box in a bright, frost-free place until 2cm (³/₄in) long sprouts grow. It can take a few weeks, but it means the spuds go into the ground already growing, which encourages fast establishment.

■ **'Earthing up'.** The process of piling soil around the stems in 15–25cm (6–10in) ridges along the rows of the plants as they grow. Do this as the stems grow to encourage more spuds to form and to bury any that are near the surface, which might otherwise turn green.

■ **'Blight'.** A fungal disease that spreads in humid, wet weather in summer, and appears as blotches on the leaves. Over time the blotches join up and spread down the stem into the crop.

■ **'Scab'.** A disease that makes potato skins rough. It is caused by dry conditions, so add plenty of moisture-holding compost to the soil before planting.

maincrops have been poor, due to blight, so I've moved away from the traditional approach of planting just the earlies in March and leaving the mid- and maincrops until April and planted them all at the same time. Although I have to protect their tops with fleece against the frost, the extra growing time in the soil means that even in a wet, blighted year, heavy crops are still produced.

My favourite spuds are earlies as they are so reliable and are up and out of the ground before the risk of serious blight attack. Plant them 40cm (16in) apart in shallow 15cm (6in) trenches, spacing the rows 50cm (20in) apart. As they grow, pile soil around the stems in stages, eventually leaving 30cm (12in) tall ridges along the rows. This process is known as 'earthing-up' and it ensures that the crop of spuds stays out of the sunlight and doesn't turn green. It also encourages more potatoes to form from the stem so your crops will be heavier. Normally earlies are ready to harvest around the time when the plant's flowers begin to open, but I start to lift them well before this in order to avoid gluts.

tip

For new potatoes at Christmas, save a few harvested new potatoes in the salad box of the fridge and replant them in late August in the greenhouse border. The tops will die down, but a harvest of small spuds will be there for lifting on Christmas Day.

The downside of earlies is that they don't keep well, so this is where maincrops come in. My favourite potatoes for chips and roasting are the classic 'King Edward' and 'Cara'. More disease-resistant varieties are 'Sante' and 'Sarpo Axona', which is practically immune to the effects of blight, although its texture is on the dry side. Plant maincrops 40cm (16in) apart, in rows 75cm (30in) apart, and second earlies, such as the scab-resistant 'Wilja', somewhere in-between – 60cm (2ft) apart.

When it comes to harvesting spuds for storage, choose a sunny day in early September, before the slugs find them, and fork the roots from the ground, leaving them on the surface for an hour or so for the skins to harden. Don't wash, but bag them up into paper or hessian sacks and store in a cool, dark, frost-free place. Any damaged spuds or those with slug damage should be eaten within a few weeks of lifting.

Growing a range of potato varieties is all part of the fun. Each year a different type will outperform the others and also, thanks to the vagaries of the weather, they will taste slightly better (or worse!) from year to year.

BEAT THE BLIGHT

■ Choose disease-resistant varieties, such as 'Sarpo Mira' and 'Cara'. Buy new sets annually rather than reuse your own. The widest range is always from mail-order seed companies, rather than the garden centre.

■ Plant potatoes early and protect them with fleece.

■ Pick off affected leaves at the first sign of attack – brown circular blotches on leaves that have a fringe of mould around them on the undersides of the leaves.

■ Spray with a copper-based fungicide when attacks are first spotted. It won't solve the problem, but it may help check the spread.

■ In severe attacks, cut down the foliage to just above the soil surface before the rot enters the stems. Leave the crop in the ground for another two weeks before lifting and storing.

■ Check stored potatoes regularly and remove any spuds that develop reddish-brown patches or signs of rot before it spreads to the others.

■ Burn or hot-compost affected material and fork as many small spuds from the soil as possible.

■ Remove self-sown tomato seedlings and 'pioneer' potato plants that grow from tiny tubers left in the ground from the previous year.

SPUDS IN TUBS

Potatoes make excellent container crops and, if grown in the greenhouse, can be ready to pick in early May. Quarter-fill a large container, at least 40cm (16in) wide and deep, with potting compost and plant 3–5 chitted earlies, such as 'Swift' or 'Rocket', just below the compost surface. Keep the container in a sunny spot and water regularly to keep the compost moist. Every couple of weeks, as the foliage grows, add more compost to bury the stems until they are 5–10cm (2–4in) below the rim of the container. When the stems start to flower, empty out the compost and harvest your spuds.

RADISHES

These are child's play to grow, just sow the seed in the sun in early spring (or from as early as January if you're sowing the seed under a cloche) or autumn, and watch them grow. They are a great crop for using up space between slower growers, such as potatoes and carrots. Of the summer varieties, my favourites are the spicy round types and 'Munchen bier', which is grown for its edible seedpods and is great for adding a kick to a stir fry.

RUNNER BEANS

Eaten straight from the garden, runner beans have an almost buttery texture, with no stringiness, and they taste so much better than any bean you can buy. I grow mine on stout 2.1m (7ft) wigwams with wide 1.2m (4ft) bases – the wider they are at the bottom, the more room there is for the crop of beans to hang down inside the supports, where they are easy to pick and shaded so they stay tender for longer. (See p.78 for how to make a wigwam.)

Push the seeds 5cm (2in) into the soil at the base of each upright. When they emerge, if they don't start to climb on their own, secure the stems with a loose loop of twine. For the biggest and best crop, good soil laced with manure and compost is essential, but keep a lookout for slugs as they will be drawn to the lush growth. When the beans 'top-out' at the summit of your supports, snip off the tops to encourage the flowers to turn into beans, and by July you will be picking every day or so.

tip

Runners grow well in semi-shade as it will make them reach up and find their own light.

Any beans that are too tough to eat (if the seeds inside are prominent through the skins the beans will be tough and stringy) can go on the compost heap. Keep picking through the summer to encourage more beans to follow, but in the autumn leave a few pods to ripen and their skins to dry. Collect the dried beans in November and keep them in airtight jars for sowing the following year. In the winter, clear away the stems, but leave the nitrogen-fixing roots for digging in to feed other crops next year. Always rotate your bean crop to prevent pests and diseases, such as leaf-notching pea and bean weevil. Prepare the soil for your next crop early by digging lots of compost and manure into the soil in late winter – the more you add, the stronger and more productive your plants will be.

SALAD LEAVES

Salads leaves are easy to grow and can be used as 'catch crops' between others to fill gaps. Most will keep coming again as you pick them, so you will have fresh salad leaves all summer long. Sow peppery rocket in late winter for picking in spring, herby mixtures of dill, coriander and Lollo lettuce for spring and summer picking, and landcress, mizuna and mustard for spicy salads in the late summer and autumn, then cover them with a cloche when the weather turns cold and pick through winter. Sow salad leaves outside in an open spot in spring and autumn, but choose a dappled, partly shady area for the summer to prevent the leaves from wilting. For lettuce plants with more solid heads, such as cos and crispheads, sow in rows from spring through to summer. Thin them out as the plants grow to leave 30cm (12in) spaces between them as they mature.

SALSIFY AND SCORZONERA

These interesting, carrot-like roots are grown in the same way as carrots, and are delicious baked in foil with butter and olive oil. Salsify has a flavour of the sea, while scorzonera is more like a parsnip, without the tanginess. You can also eat the flower buds of salsify (fried). Scorzonera is perennial and will keep its place in the kitchen garden if all else fails. Sow them outside in the spring as you would for carrots and expect a crop from midsummer onwards.

tip

Salsify spreads around by seed and can be invasive so pick off the fluffy round globes before they ripen.

SPINACH AND CHARD

True spinach does best from an early spring sowing, either directly into the soil or into plug trays. I grow it in blocks in raised beds in my greenhouse. Make sure that the roots never dry out, otherwise the leaves lose their tangy flavour and the plants run to seed. Chards, also called perpetual spinach, are less fussy, and although their flavour isn't quite as good as spinach, they make really welcome winter crops. All types of spinach can be harvested as cut-and-come-again crops.

SWEET CORN

Sow angular sweet corn seeds individually in 8cm (3in) pots, or in cell trays, and grow them on in a greenhouse or on a windowsill until the risk of frost has passed. The F1 varieties (see p.103) are so reliable that you can ignore the old rule about sowing two seeds per pot and pinching one out.

Plant out in a sunny spot about 30cm (12in) wide. Plant in blocks so the pollen from the tassel-like male flowers drops onto the female flowers among the leaves below. Harvest your cobs in late summer when the silky tassels at the ends of the cobs turn brown. The lower cobs will mature first, but before picking check them for ripeness by peeling back the leaves and pushing your thumb into a kernel. If the juice is milky, twist the cob from the stems. If not, push the leaves back over the cob and leave it a little longer.

tip

Look out for 'Xtra sweet varieties', they have so much sugar that they are even delicious eaten raw. Sow a couple of batches of plants between April and late June for a supply of sweet corn throughout the summer.

OUTSIDE TOMATOES

Although technically a fruit, most people consider them to be more of a vegetable. There are hundreds of varieties, but they fall into two basic groups – those for growing in the greenhouse and those that will crop outside. See p.187 for the greenhouse varieties, but here I will concentrate on those that can be grown outside.

When it comes to outdoor varieties there are some classics such as 'Red Alert, 'Gardener's Delight' and trailing 'Tumbler' that can be grown in hanging baskets. Both greenhouse and outside varieties need to be started off in a greenhouse or propagator as they won't survive cold and frosts. Start seeds off in 8cm (3in) pots around late March to early April, then prick

TOP LEFT: Chard, a beauty on the winter plot.

TOP RIGHT: Plant sweetcorn in blocks to ensure pollination.

BOTTOM LEFT: Nip side shoots from cordon tomatoes to direct energy away from the leaves and into the fruit.

BOTTOM RIGHT: Recycle plastic water bottles as cane-tops to protect your eyes when harvesting.

VEGETABLES TO BUY AS PLANTS

Raising your own vegetable plants from seed isn't always the most efficient way to grow your own. Some vegetables require the tropical heat of a propagator to sprout, and a long, cosseted growing season in a greenhouse to bear fruit. If you can't provide these essentials, then buying ready-grown plants is the answer, and a way of side stepping the work. Plus, if you wait until after the frosts, the best way to raise tender vegetables is in pots on the patio. It works for me, especially for expensive plants that you don't need many of, such as black aubergines that all have a similar flavour. Although you won't find the range of varieties that are available to buy as seed, the cost of a couple of small plants is often comparable to a packet of expensive F1 seed; so don't ever feel guilty, think of it as adopting rather than cheating…

■ **Aubergines.** These demand heat, a greenhouse and a long growing season to crop well.

■ **Chilli peppers.** Are often sold in interesting varieties and are a great pot-plant for the patio.

■ **Bell peppers.** Like aubergines, bell peppers also need a long growing season.

■ **Cucumbers.** You don't need many plants to fill a greenhouse, so it is more economical to buy plants rather than packs of F1 seed.

■ **Tomatoes.** These are relatively cheap and can be bought large and ready to crop outdoors.

■ **Winter cabbages.** It is easy to forget to sow these in late spring, and buying plants is often the best option if you are stuck for growing space until their June and July planting time.

out individual plants into 8cm (3in) pots and grow them on inside. Pot on into 12cm (5in) pots when roots appear through the holes in the bottom, and in May start to harden off plants by putting them outside during the day and bringing them in at night (see p.106). Once the risk of frost has passed the tomato plants can be planted outside, preferably in a sheltered place.

I tend to grow cordons (which means only allowing one stem to grow by pinching off the side-shoots as they appear), and train them to canes. When the pea-sized tomatoes appear, start feeding the plants once a fortnight with a high-potash tomato fertilizer. The fruits are ready to pick when the skins are soft to touch and the tomato comes away easily from the stalk.

tip

For the most flavoursome tomatoes, I water the plants in the morning and pick the fruit in the evening so that the sugars are more concentrated and the taste is better.

HERITAGE VEGETABLES

Old, heirloom vegetable varieties have been around for years, but fell from many major seed lists, almost becoming lost. Growing them not only keeps their stocks alive, thereby contributing to diversity, but can also introduce you to a wide range of old and unusual varieties with some with unique flavours. Often these old varieties are only suited to specific parts of the country; you can find this out from the supplier. Many come with fascinating histories, such as the delicious climbing French bean called Cherokee Trail of Tears, which was taken by the Cherokee tribe when they were driven from their Southern US homeland. Others, such as Black Russian and Cream Sausage tomatoes, may not be as reliable as modern types, but their flavour and appearance, as their names indicate, is quite unlike that of other tomatoes. You are unlikely to find many heritage varieties in garden centres, so it is best to seek out suppliers that specialize in heritage varieties.

FEEDING

The best way to feed vegetables is to increase the natural fertility of the soil by forking in garden compost or well-rotted manure in winter, before the growing season starts. Manure is ideal for hungry crops such as potatoes and brassicas, but if it is in short supply spread general fertilizer pellets amongst the rows at planting and again when the crops are harvested to boost nutrient levels for the crops that follow on afterwards. Tomatoes, chillies and peppers that are grown in pots benefit from a high-potash liquid feed, applied every fortnight from when their fruit starts to set – bottles of concentrate can be bought from garden centres or you can make your own from comfrey leaves, see p.86. As well as forking in compost I also feed plants throughout the season with liquid seaweed fertilizer. It contains minerals and minor nutrients and can really make a difference to the health of the plants.

VEGETABLE SOWING PLANNER A–Z

Vegetable type	Jan	Feb	March	April	May	June	July	Aug	Sept	Oct	Nov	Dec
Artichoke (Chinese)			▓	▓	▓							
Artichoke (globe)			▓	▓	▓							
Artichoke (Jerusalem)	▓	▓	▓	▓							▓	▓
Asparagus		▓	▓	▓								
Asparagus (pea)				▓	▓							
Aubergine		▓	▓	▓	▓							
Beetroot		▓	▓	▓	▓	▓	▓					
Broad bean		▓	▓	▓	▓						▓	
Broccoli (chinese)						▓	▓	▓				
Broccoli (sprouting)				▓	▓							
Brussels sprouts			▓	▓								
Chinese cabbage						▓	▓	▓	▓			
Cabbage (red)			▓	▓	▓							
Cabbage (spring)								▓	▓			
Cabbage (summer & autumn)			▓	▓	▓							
Cabbage (winter)				▓	▓							
Calabrese				▓	▓	▓	▓	▓	▓			
Carrots		▓	▓	▓	▓	▓	▓	▓				
Cauliflower (early autumn)			▓	▓	▓							
Cauliflower (winter)				▓	▓							
Celeriac		▓	▓									
Celery			▓	▓								
Corn salad				▓	▓	▓	▓	▓				
Cucumber				▓	▓	▓						
Endive			▓	▓	▓	▓	▓	▓	▓			
Florence fennel						▓	▓					
French bean				▓	▓	▓	▓					
Garlic		▓	▓							▓	▓	

grow outdoor varieties plant directly in to veg beds

heavy soil   sandy soil

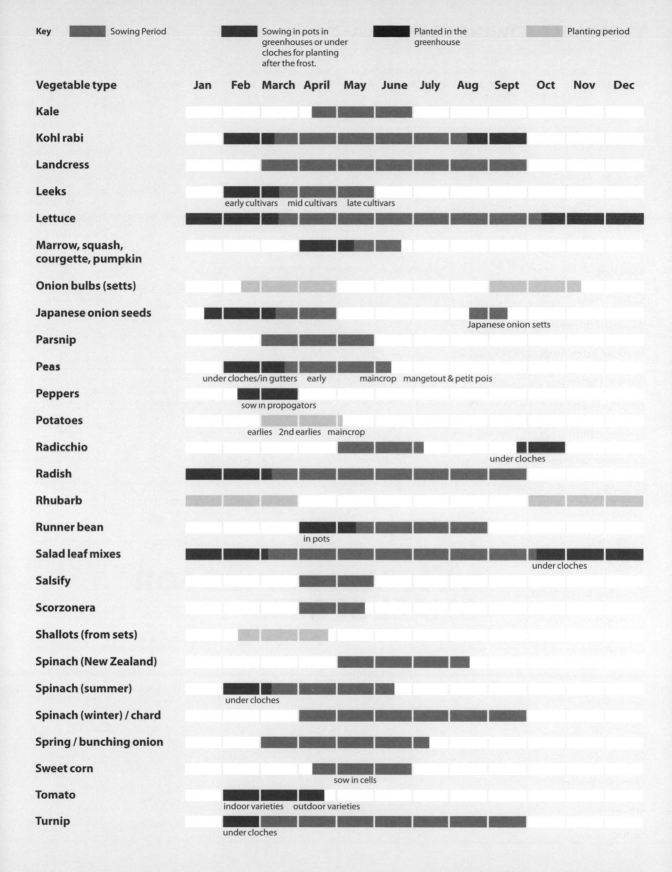

Key — Sowing Period | Sowing in pots in greenhouses or under cloches for planting after the frost. | Planted in the greenhouse | Planting period

Vegetable type	Jan	Feb	March	April	May	June	July	Aug	Sept	Oct	Nov	Dec
Kale												
Kohl rabi												
Landcress												
Leeks												
Lettuce												
Marrow, squash, courgette, pumpkin												
Onion bulbs (setts)												
Japanese onion seeds												
Parsnip												
Peas												
Peppers												
Potatoes												
Radicchio												
Radish												
Rhubarb												
Runner bean												
Salad leaf mixes												
Salsify												
Scorzonera												
Shallots (from sets)												
Spinach (New Zealand)												
Spinach (summer)												
Spinach (winter) / chard												
Spring / bunching onion												
Sweet corn												
Tomato												
Turnip												

Chart annotations:
- Leeks: early cultivars — mid cultivars — late cultivars
- Japanese onion seeds: Japanese onion setts
- Peas: under cloches/in gutters — early — maincrop — mangetout & petit pois
- Peppers: sow in propogators
- Potatoes: earlies — 2nd earlies — maincrop
- Radicchio: under cloches
- Runner bean: in pots
- Salad leaf mixes: under cloches
- Spinach (summer): under cloches
- Sweet corn: sow in cells
- Tomato: indoor varieties — outdoor varieties
- Turnip: under cloches

CROPS FOR VEGETABLES GRIDS

■ **Salad leaves and herbs including rocket, parsley, chervil, loose-leaf lettuce and basil.** Broadcast liberally in each square and grow as cut-and-come-again crops.

■ **Radishes.** Grow 16 plants per 30 x 30cm (1 x 1ft) square for roots or two 'Rats Tail' types at the back of the bed for seed pods.

■ **Nantes carrots.** Broadcast in 60 x 60cm (2 x 2ft) blocks and thin to 40 equally spaced plants as they grow.

■ **Turnips.** I find fast, small, Japanese types the best. Sow 16 plants per 30 x 30cm (1 x 1ft) square.

■ **Beetroot.** Plant 40–50 per 60 x 60cm (2 x 2ft) square and thin as they grow or broadcast for baby leaves.

■ **Chinese cabbage.** Sow four per 30 x 30cm (1 x 1ft) square, or multi-sow for cut-and-come-again leaves.

■ **Summer cabbage.** Sow six plants per 60 x 60cm (2 x 2ft) square.

■ **Leeks.** Grow baby leeks, planting 50 in a 30 x 60cm (1 x 2ft) rectangle.

■ **Kohlrabi.** Sow 18 per 60 x 60cm (2 x 2ft) square.

■ **Dwarf French beans.** Grow in 30 x 120cm (1 x 4ft) blocks, planting two rows down the middle and spacing the plants 10cm (4in) apart.

■ **Tomatoes.** One plant per 30 x 30cm (1 x 1ft) square for cordon types at the back of the bed, or one trailer at the front with its stems trained over the edge.

■ **Chilli peppers.** One per 30 x 30cm (1 x 1ft) square.

■ **Peas.** Grow sugar-snaps and mange tout up pea-sticks in 30 x 120cm (1 x 4ft) strips.

■ **Dwarf runner beans.** Grow as for peas.

VEGETABLE GRIDS FOR SMALL SPACES

Also known as 'square-foot gardening', this is when small blocks of vegetables are grown next to each other for maximum crops in a small space. Ideally, do this in a raised bed as marking out, patrolling for slugs and re-sowing are easier. Use string and pegs to divide the bed into equal-sized plots and sow or plant between the string lines. The divisions can be as small as 30 x 30cm (1 x 1ft) for salads, although I find 60 x 60cm (2 x 2ft) squares or 30 x 120cm (1 x 4ft) rectangles more productive for roots and beans. After a crop is cleared, feed the soil with a general fertilizer and re-sow immediately with another crop.

CULINARY HERBS TO GROW

These are my favourite, and I think most useful, kitchen herbs. Grow them close to the kitchen door so they are quick and easy to pick while you are cooking. They all live from year to year, unlike annual herbs that need sowing afresh every spring.

ROSEMARY

This classic evergreen herb will thrive in a sunny spot with free-draining soil – it always does well in the typically dry spot that most people have next to the brickwork of the house. There are many different varieties, but the best for cooking is the run-of-the-mill species *Rosmarinus officinalis*. Some of the shorter leaved varieties can be a bit medicinal-smelling, whereas this long-leaved type is sweet and tangy. Rosemary is great with bacon, tomatoes, roast potatoes and lamb.

OREGANO AND MARJORAM

I grow oregano on the edge of a sunny raised bed where it's well drained and up high for easy picking. It is a spreading

herbaceous plant that dies down in winter, although even then there are always small clusters of leaves to gather from the crown. There are dozens of varieties, but my favourite is golden marjoram. To ensure a fresh supply of leaves through summer trim it back with the secateurs when it starts to flower to encourage another flush of tasty growth. Oregano is a great herb for roast chicken, pizza and minced meat on the barbecue.

FENNEL

Fennel is a very accommodating and ornamental herb which will add a soft, see-through quality to your borders. The best flavour comes from growing it in a hot, dry place, as this makes the aniseed-flavoured, feathery leaves even more oily and intense. Finely chop and sprinkle fennel on top of salmon before cooking, or use it to stuff whole mackerels before barbecuing them. Fennel seeds add an anise flavour to winter casseroles.

MINT

Mint doesn't like hot, dry places and is quite happy in semi-shade, which means it is a good plant for behind the shed where little else will grow and where its spreading roots won't get mixed up with other perennials. I grow a few different types of mint in boxed beds, to contain their invasive roots, on the shady side of my greenhouse. Spearmint is best for peas and potatoes, with its clean flavour, whereas apple mint is delicious in Pimm's, and in taste tests nine out of ten of my friends said they preferred Moroccan mint in a mojito. Chop plants back when they flower in summer to encourage a flush of fresh growth, and again in winter when they go to ground.

TARRAGON

I grow tarragon next to my oregano because it also likes the free-draining soil of a raised bed. Like oregano, it is a spreading, herbaceous plant, but it isn't that hardy so I mulch over the crowns when they have died down in winter to keep off the frosts. In summer the leaves add a mild fennel flavour to chicken and make creamy sauces less cloying. French tarragon is far better for flavour; Russian tarragon is just a bit of a thug.

tip

Thyme is long-lived in perfect, free-draining, Mediterranean conditions, but in our climate it tends to get leggy if it is not regularly trimmed and plants are prone to dying in winter. So take semi-ripe cuttings (see p.115) to propagate, or buy a new plant every couple of years.

SAGE

Of all herbs sage is the most ornamental, with evergreen leaves and a sprawling habit that makes it an ideal softener for the edge of a sunny border. There's little to choose from in terms of flavour, but for looks I like purple sage and the silver-leaved common sage best. I use it laid over a chicken breast and wrapped in foil before roasting in the oven, or chopped up finely with chestnuts, breadcrumbs and egg for a homemade stuffing.

THYME

Thyme, with its powerful flavour, is the herb for cooking with beef – a few sprigs added to a hearty winter casserole will give it a delicious tang. Thyme is a low-growing spreader and, depending on the variety, will form mats or cushions if given full sun and free-draining soil. I grow two types, Lemon and Silver Queen, in the same pot so their contrasting leaves make a tapestry of silver and gold. The ordinary *Thymus officinalis* has the best flavour for cooking, in my book.

tip

Soft annual herbs, such as dill, basil and coriander, will keep for months in the freezer. Just cut off the stems, wrap them whole in tin foil and lay them on the freezer shelf for a fresh summery taste throughout the winter.

CULINARY HERBS TO SOW

Annual herbs are just like bedding plants and need to be sown every year in spring (see p.99), then if they flower and peter out sow them again in early summer. Plant them out in well-lit window boxes, containers on the patio or sunny borders where they are easy to reach for picking and regular watering.

BASIL

This is a real sun lover so don't bother sowing it until May. Sow it in pots or trays in the greenhouse or on a sunny windowsill indoors, then plant it out in direct sun in a warm, sheltered spot after the risk of frost has passed. 'Sweet Genovese' or the smaller-leaved 'Minette' are best for salads. There are also more colourful lemon and Thai versions, but I find the flavours a bit too much like liquorice for my taste. Basil is delicious with tomatoes – and will happily grow around their feet in a greenhouse border.

CORIANDER

Sow this directly outside in rows on a sunny allotment or vegetable patch from April onwards, or as a permanent self-sowing crop in the greenhouse for pickings from late winter through until late autumn. The best variety is the regular 'Cilantro', which is slower to bolt to flower. Corianders must be kept moist when they are growing and should not be transplanted or they will bolt. Freshly cut leaves are delicious in salads, or as a final splash of fresh green taste in home-cooked curries.

PARSLEY

This is the perfect crop for pots and vegetable beds that are in sun or semi-shade. There are two types of parsley. The French flat-leaved type likes to grow in slightly warmer temperatures and has a softer, some say better, flavour. The curly type will survive a mild frost and is traditionally used as a dark-green garnish, but is also great for blending into sauces. I pick the leaves by the handful and blend them with garlic, olive oil and lemon juice to make a salsa verde paste that is lovely on salmon.

DILL

This is a very easy annual to grow and can be liberally scattered wherever there is a bare patch on the vegetable patch or allotment. It quickly goes to flower in dry weather, but that doesn't matter as you can also eat the flowers and it won't spoil the taste. It has a lovely fine anise flavour that is perfect with fish.

GUIDE TO POPULAR FRUIT

APPLES

There are many varieties of apple – dessert, cookers and crab apple. My advice is to choose varieties that were bred or originated in your region, as they will be naturally adapted to the local weather and will be less likely to succumb to pests and diseases. The West Country, where I live, isn't ideal for growing apples because the moist maritime air makes the fruit prone to scab, a fungal disease that creates unappetising black marks

RIGHT: 'Kidd's Orange Red' is one of my favourite apples. It's red and sugary, yet tart – rather like a Cox, but easier to grow outside of the sunny south-east, so a good one for gardeners in the North.

on the fruit. You are more likely to find cider apples, known for their high-tannin content and sun-ripened sugary-sweet flavour, rather than blemish-free dessert apples that grow best in the sunny south-east where the air is drier and the sunshine more reliable. But even in Devon it is possible to grow scab-free apples, such as 'Sunset', 'Ashmead's Kernel' and russets with their thicker skins that are less prone to disease. Look to your local tree-fruit nurseries for the best advice.

Plant apples trees in the autumn so they can establish their roots and will be less reliant on you watering them the following summer. See p.164 for information on rootstocks.

See p.164 for information on rootstocks.

tip

Give fruit bushes and trained trees a boost once they've finished fruiting with a potassium-rich fertilizer, then water well and mulch round the stems with compost from your heap.

MAKE A FRUIT CAGE

Fruit cages are great for keeping the birds off your soft fruit. Although you can buy them from garden centres, you can save a fortune by making your own. My favourite fruit-cage shape is a 'tent', made from a rectangle of uprights for the corners and a taller pole in the centre.

1 Openable net to allow birds in to pick over plants in the winter

2 U-shaped nails fix the net to the batons

3 Door

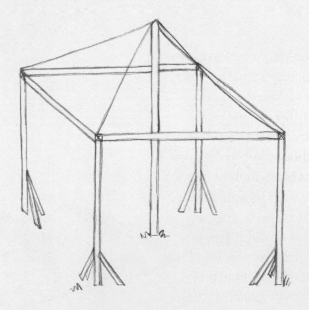

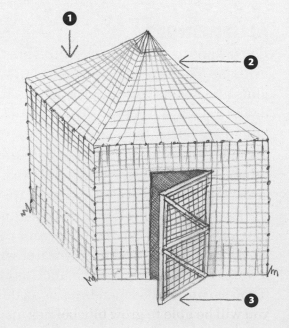

BLACKCURRANTS

Blackcurrants are one of the easiest fruit crops to grow. Buy them as potted or bare-rooted bushes and plant in the autumn in a sunny spot. I grow the relatively compact 'Ben Sarek'.

Unlike other fruits that are best grown on a single stem, blackcurrants yield more fruit if they are grown as a thicket. To encourage lots of growth from below ground level, plant them in rich, well-composted soil, set 5cm (2in) deeper than the old soil line in the pot – this buries the bottom buds and encourages them to root. In the first winter, prune the stems down to about 5cm (2in) above the ground. Although this will rob you of a few berries in the first summer, the larger plant it creates in the second summer will be well worth the wait. Once the plant is established, keep it vigorous by pruning back a quarter of the older wood (distinguishable by its grey colour) down to the base.

During the growing season keep an eye on the leaves, if they appear distorted it is probably aphids, so pinch or wash off affected leaves with a hose. If leaves appear rounded or an odd shape, it's probably a virus called 'reversion'. This is caused by a tiny insect called the big bud mite that makes the buds swell, but not open. Prune off any affected stems and burn them, or if plants are very badly affected you may have to destroy the whole bush and start again.

BLUEBERRIES

If you want to grow fruit in containers then blueberries are brilliant. They produce berries over a long period, which avoids gluts and means you can pick just a few purple marbles every day to top off your muesli. There are a few different varieties, but all are bush-shaped and can grow to between 90cm (3ft) and 2m (6ft) tall. 'Bluecrop' is an easy-to-grow classic, which is very reliable and pest-free. Always buy two plants because blueberries crop more in company, even though they are sold as self-fertile.

Plant up in a container of compost and put them in full or part-day sun. You can use ericaceous compost or John Innes No 3, but it is essential to only water with rainwater from a water butt as they hate the lime in tap water. Alternatively, if you can grow rhododendrons or azaleas in your garden, then you will be able to grow blueberries just as easily in a border.

ROOTSTOCKS

If you buy your fruit tree from a nursery the top part of the tree will probably have been grafted onto different roots, or rootstock. This is done to enable younger plants to grow more vigorously and to produce fruit faster. You choose the rootstock according to the space you have in your garden, as this will determine how large the tree will grow.

Apples:

■ **M27.** Very dwarfing, 60cm–1.2m (6–4ft). Good for container-grown trees.

■ **M9.** Dwarfing, 2.5–2.75m (8–9ft). Ideal for training cordons and espaliers.

■ **M26.** Dwarfing, 2.5–3.5m (8–12ft). For training or a small garden tree.

■ **MM106.** Semi-dwarfing, 3.5–4m (12–13ft). Good for small orchards and allotments.

■ **MM111.** Vigorous, 4–4.5m (13–15ft). Medium to large gardens and orchards.

■ **M25.** Very vigorous, 4.5x6m (15x20ft). Medium to large gardens and orchards.

Pears:

■ **Quince C**. Dwarfing, 2–3m (6–10ft). Bush or cordon.

■ **Quince.** Semi-vigorous, 3–4.5m (10–15ft). Bush, espalier, fan or half-standard tree.

Cherries:

■ **Gisela or G5.** Semi-dwarfing, 2.5–3m (8–10ft). Bush or fan-trained tree.

■ **Colt.** Semi-vigorous, 6m (20ft) trees.

Plums, damsons, greengages:

■ **Pixy.** Semi-dwarfing, 3–3.5m (10–12ft). Cordon or bush.

■ **Saint Julien A.** Semi-vigorous, 4.5–5.5m (14–18ft). Fan-trained or bush.

CHERRIES

There is something very special about harvesting cherries – it must be the associations I have with abundance and good times. I have a sweet, self-fertile 'Stella' on my allotment and even though I only pick a handful each time I visit in June and July I always feel it's a great treat.

Cherry trees can be bought on small rootstocks called 'Colt' that restrict the size to 3–5m (12–16ft). This means that you can net part or all the tree to protect the fruit from hungry birds. You can also restrict the size by pruning the soft summer growth back by half, but only do this on a dry day in the summer to avoid the risk of silver leaf fungus spores infecting it. Cherries like full sun and good soil, and it is worth mulching around the trunk of the tree to keep the weeds down until the tree is established. It is also important to protect the flowers from frost, so when it is in blossom drape fleece over the tree if cold weather is predicted.

FIGS

Figs are a good crop for sunny city gardens where the warmth of the surrounding buildings helps the fruit to ripen. I know urban gardeners who get bucket loads of plump, sugary 'Brown Turkey' (the hardiest variety), even in semi-shaded plots.

Normally figs only fruit when the plants reach tree-like proportions, but they can be tricked into earlier production by planting the roots in a large container constructed from paving slabs set on edge into the soil. As long as the slabs are sunk 45cm (1½ft) in the soil the roots can't escape and soon fill the container, slowing the plant's growth, which encourages it to bear fruit.

If you have a fig tree that won't fruit, prune back the new, green-stemmed summer shoots in August to five leaves. This will encourage pea-sized embryonic fruits to grow where the leaves meet the stem. They will over winter and swell to picking size the following summer. Harvest the fruit when the skins are soft and a dewdrop of sugary sap appears at the base.

GOOSEBERRIES

The first gooseberries that swell in June have a lovely, sharp tartness, but leave them on the bush until midsummer and they grow into soft, sweet orbs that are reminiscent of kiwi fruit. You can plant gooseberries at any time of the year, either as pot-grown plants or more economically in winter as a bare-root bush. Add lots of compost to the soil, as they don't like stony or poor soil, and keep them watered in dry summers.

The trick with gooseberries is to keep on top of the pruning – if it is left to its own devices a gooseberry bush will form an impenetrable thicket of thorny branches that makes picking a scratchy, painful business. The close-quarter conditions of an unpruned bush also gives air little room to circulate and leads to leaf-destroying American mildew fungal disease. When pruning, remove congested branches from the centre of the bush to allow in light and to encourage new growth that will carry fruit next season. You need to prune twice a year – once in the winter, to remove congested and low branches, and once in the summer, to remove overenthusiastic stems that crowd the middle of the plant. Watch out for caterpillar-like sawfly larvae which will

strip the plant of leaves in days. Remove them by hand or spray the bush with a nematode caterpillar killer (see p.226).

GRAPE VINES

Grape vines are vigorous climbers that are perfect for training over a sun-soaked pergola or arch. They grow in all but damp soils, even where the earth is thin and stony, but must have sun for the fruit to ripen. The most reliable variety in the UK is 'Seyval Blanc', which bears heavy crops of white, seeded grapes that ripen early.

For good-quality grapes you can't be shy with your secateurs! pruning and thinning are essential and there are many different ways to do it. After planting, train one or two main stems up your arch or pergola or wires. Trim them back to the older dark wood, roughly 40cm (16in) above the ground, in the winter. When growth starts again in the summer, train one or two new shoots back up the support and trim the first flush of side-shoots back to five leaves (these should be spaced 50cm (20in) apart up the stem). This pruning will trigger a second flush of growth that you can snip back to a single leaf.

By shortening these shoots, the remaining stems ripen and instead of buds that turn into leaves, fruit buds form near the stem on what are known as fruiting spurs. Bunches of grapes will then form from the growth that appears on the spurs every summer. In winter, prune the growth back to two buds from the spurs and each summer train the fruit-bearing side-shoots that grow from them up the supports.

PEACHES, APRICOTS AND NECTARINES

The warming climate has made these seemingly exotic fruits ever easier to grow. It was never the cold damaging the trees that was the problem, it was that they flower early in the year when few bees are around to pollinate them and frosts are still a threat to their delicate shell-pink blooms.

Traditionally they have always been planted against a south- or west-facing wall. The extra warmth helps the fruits ripen in summer, while in spring it allows you to pin up plastic over the wall-trained branches as protection from frost damage and fungal diseases on peaches. Peach leaf curl is a disease that

LEFT: Ouch! Never mind the pain, think of the taste! The longer you leave gooseberries to ripen the more kiwi-like their flavour becomes.

PRUNING AND TRAINING FRUIT TREES

Fruit trees don't need pruning, they will happily grow and crop if left to their own devices. However, regular trimming encourages the trees to bear fruit from a younger age and reduces the tree's size, so more varieties can be grown in a small space.

Pruning is also a way of reducing fungal diseases, such as mildew and scab, which can distort and scar foliage and fruit. It also reinvigorates tired old trees, encouraging new growth. On previously un-trimmed, established trees aim to keep the centre open by removing branches that cross or rub against each other and any crowded twiggy growth. This aids air circulation and prevents fungal spores from getting a toe hold.

Apples, apricots, pears, gooseberries red and white currants all respond particularly well to pruning and training into fans and espaliers and are ideal for growing along wires fixed to walls and fences. Strong and vigorous main branches should be selected and tied to bamboo canes that are in turn secured to wires. These branches are tied in

as they grow, while the rest are pruned away. Between July and August, cut back the soft growth that sprouts from the sides of the main branches by two-thirds. If shoots grow from side shoots or spurs formed in previous years (you can spot these as their base is thicker and bear a cluster of leaves), cut them back to 2.5cm (1in) above the old growth. As well as keeping the tree trimmed and in shape, summer pruning encourages the base of the cut stems to 'ripen' into fruiting spurs close to the main branches. In autumn, follow up by trimming any re-growth back to 2cm ($^3/_4$in) from the main branches.

To grow your own cordons, fans or espaliers, choose semi-dwarfing rootstocks and varieties that fruit on spurs (short, flower-bearing twigs that grow close to the main stem). Pears and most apples are spur-fruiting, although 'Worcester Pearmain', the cooker 'Bramley's Seedling', 'Discovery' and 'Lord Lambourne' are all exceptions that fruit on the branch tips and so are best grown as free-standing trees.

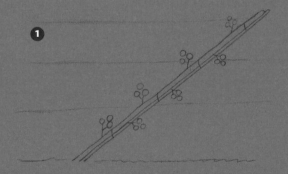

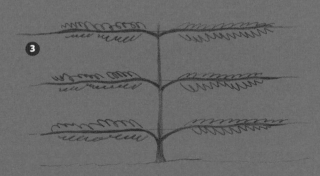

1 Cordon training is space-efficient and good for growing lots of types of apples, white and red currants, and gooseberries.

2 Fan-training is ideal for apricots, cherries and peaches.

3 Espalier is formal and romantic. It's great for pears and apples.

attacks the leaves as they emerge from the stems, causing them to blister and twist. Incidentally, exciting new developments in America and Canada have brought about tougher apricot plants that are suitable for more northern gardens. Nurserymen have suggested that these are better planted on an east-facing wall – something I'm experimenting with on a 'Goldcott' at Greenacre – as the flowers bloom later and are therefore less liable to frost damage. Whichever aspect you choose, the most reliable and easy-to-protect crops are from trees trained as fans onto wires on a wall or fence at least 2m (6ft) high, and pruned in summer to keep growth in bounds.

Peaches and nectarines fruit on last year's wood and are pruned after fruiting to remove the fruited shoots. Apricots are pruned like pears on spurs. The removal of larger branches every four years is necessary on all of these trees to encourage new growth. To ensure pollination, rub a small brush between the flowers when they emerge and keep the soil moist as the fruit swells. Mulch the soil around the tree every spring.

Always prune to buds that face out from the centre of a plant, so that subsequent shoots grow outwards. This helps air movement through the branches and helps to keep fruit and leaves disease-free, plus the horizontal re-growth bears more fruit than branches.

PEARS

Pears grow really well in clay soil, and should literally come in pairs as, apart from the variety 'Concord', they need a partner to pollinate them. This may not be a problem if there is already a pear tree nearby, so take a look around your allotment or a peek into your neighbour's gardens.

Like all tree fruit, they are best planted in the autumn and are available on different rootstocks (see p.164) which will control the eventual size of the tree. If your garden is cold, buy a dwarfing rootstock and grow it cordon-trained against a fence or wall to protect it from the frost. Harvest pears when the stalk comes away from the tree with a gentle twist.

PLUMS

Plums are one of the most abundant fruit crops in the garden, in fact almost too abundant, as the tendency for branches to break under the weight of fruit testifies! This is a particular problem with the popular 'Victoria', so it always pays to thin out some of the swelling fruit or prop up the heavy branches with stout stakes.

Plum trees are early to flower, which means frosts can destroy all hope of a crop, so plant in a sheltered part of the garden away from cold winds and frost pockets. Ideally, plant in autumn and add lots of compost or well-rotted manure to the planting hole, particularly if your soil is shallow, sandy or chalky.

In spring, buy a pheromone trap and hang it in the tree to trap plum moth maggots, w hich will spoil your fruit. Leave the tree to its own devices, but if you do prune, never do it in winter as this is when the spores of the deadly silver leaf fungus (which will infect the cuts and spread through the tree), are about.

RASPBERRIES

Easy to grow and happy in part-shade, 'razzers' are the perfect crop for the bottom of the garden next to the shed. There are lots of different varieties, but only two types: ones that fruit in summer and ones that fruit in the autumn. If you have space, plant both, but keep them apart as they need different pruning.

Autumn varieties produce fruit on the current season's growth and need to be pruned to the ground after fruiting in order to fruit the following year. Summer fruiters need to overwinter as canes so the ones that have already fruited can be cut back while new wood is tied to wires for next year's crop.

Garden centres sell raspberry plants as canes (bare-root, dead-looking sticks) by the bundle in late autumn. You can also buy established, potted plants for a higher price. The best way to grow raspberries is to plant them in rows 45cm (18in) apart, with 1m (40in) between the rows for easy picking. Plant them in soil that has been improved with garden compost or well-rotted manure. Chop the canes just above a bud down to around 30cm (12in) above the ground and a sturdy post in at the end of each row with wires running between them to allow you to tie in the canes up with soft twine. Keep raspberry plants well mulched with compost.

RHUBARB

Plant rhubarb in the winter in a sunny spot in improved soil, making sure all the weeds have been cleared first. If the soil is heavy clay, plant the bulbous-red buds just above the soil surface to help with drainage, or if the soil is light sand

RIGHT: The fleece and bin goes over my rhubarb in early January and you can start picking the blanched and tender stems in February.

or chalk, plant just below the soil so the roots get more moisture.

To get an early spring harvest, force stems to start growing in midwinter by placing a 15cm (6in) layer of straw over the crown and cover it with an upturned pot or dustbin. You should be pulling (don't slice or snap!) super-tender stems within a few weeks. Alternatively, harvest stems naturally in spring and summer, but stop picking from mid-summer as the stems are thin and stringy after then.

Give the plant a boost with a high-nitrogen feed, such as chicken manure pellets, and mulch around the stems in autumn with compost or well-rotted manure.

STRAWBERRIES

What better place to be in summer than a strawberry patch? Start your strawberry patch with about a dozen plants in spring or autumn. Look for plants that are labelled as 'virus-free' to be sure of good, disease-free stock. Plant them in rows about 45cm (18in) in soil that has been improved with lots of compost. They will grow in part-day shade or with other taller soft-fruit plants, such as a gooseberry bush.

Put some straw or newspaper weighed down with bark chippings under the trusses of swelling fruit to keep them clean and slug-free. When they are red and juicy, pick them

MATCH YOUR FRUIT AND VEGETABLES TO YOUR SOIL TYPE

■ **Clay soil.** The best crops for clay soils are brassicas, but check the pH and lime if necessary. Warm the soil up before sowing with cloches and don't dig when it's wet. If the soil is soggy, even in summer, mound the soil up into raised beds to improve the drainage. Provided you improve the drainage with plenty of organic matter and compost, all vegetables and fruit will grow well in clay soil.

■ **Sandy soil.** Quick to warm up in spring, but also to dry out in summer, sand is ideal for carrots and parsnips. If compost is added beetroot grows well too, as do globe artichokes, onions, garlic beans winter and early salad crops. New sowing and plantings dry out fast in hot weather so you'll need to keep an eye on watering. As nutrients are quickly leached out, look for signs of hunger – yellowing leaves and short growth – and feed with blood, fish and bone. Sandy soils tend to be acidic so blueberries grow well, although liming/

improving with spent mushroom compost will be necessary to grow brassicas.

■ **Chalky soil.** This type of soil tends to be shallow so it can be difficult to grow fruit, which prefers deep, rich soils. Brassicas, sweet corn, salads, onions, parsnips and scab-resistant potatoes will all grow well in chalky soils that have been improved with lots of composts, as will cherry trees. Chalk soil can be dry and hungry, so water regularly and feed often with comfrey teas and seaweed feeds. Feed with blood, fish and bone when crops are replaced and mulch around spring plantings to trap in moisture.

■ **Silt.** This is similar to clay, although it can be more quickly improved than clay with the addition of organic matter and compost. The choice of plants you can grow is the same as clay, as is the proviso not to cultivate when it is wet. Raised beds improve the drainage and mean you can grow early crops such as salads.

between your finger and thumb, taking the green stalk too as this prevents moulds from forming on the plants. After picking all the strawberries, snip off all of the foliage and clear the straw from around the plants to reduce the chances of disease.

You will notice that the plant makes runners (baby plants) that sprawl out from the central plant, but the first year after planting it is best to remove and compost these so as not to weaken the main plant while it establishes. In subsequent years, however, the strongest runners can be cut off and planted, but not on land that has grown strawberries in the last five years as it could still harbour pests and diseases. Because strawberries crop best in the second and third year after planting, propagate a few runners every year to guarantee a constant supply. Dig out and compost parent plants as they become less productive, usually after their fourth crop.

GET A GREEN-HOUSE

I didn't buy my first greenhouse, it came with the house I was renting at the time – in fact the greenhouse was one of the reasons I rented the house. The 1930s terrace was nothing special, but the sight of the small glass structure, slightly tumbledown with a few broken panes of glass, tucked away at the back of the garden spoke to me of opportunity and plenty.

When you are renting a property you don't want to spend money on plants that you will eventually have to leave behind, which is why I got into sowing annuals. The first summer I turned half the garden over to zinnia, French marigolds and sunflowers. In front of them I planted all sorts of vegetables – beetroots, peas, carrots and endless salad leaves – all reared in the greenhouse and planted out. The year after that, there was less work to do as many of the flowers self-seeded, coming up in new places and filling the garden with colour and buzzing bees. This gave me time to experiment with more vegetables and to really put the greenhouse to use.

Since then I've never been without a greenhouse; it is the powerhouse for my garden, my allotment and my kitchen. Although you can use them to house pot plants, such as orchids or alpines, all year round, I am more interested in using the greenhouse to generate plants for the vegetable plot, as well as a few cut flowers and companion plants. Using the greenhouse to start off your vegetables in cell-trays and pots steals a march on the season, as you won't need to wait for cleared ground to get started. They say men love their sheds, but for me it's my greenhouse – a productive sanctuary to escape to with my seeds and wind-up radio to listen to the footie.

GREENHOUSES

Greenhouses come in an array of types and styles – metal framed and wood framed in a range of sizes and shapes, including unusual geodesic domes. But whichever you choose, even if it's just the cheapest, rectangular, aluminium-framed type, it will vastly increase what you can grow in your garden.

More expensive, but better looking, are the wooden-framed greenhouses that tend to be warmer and are good for growing winter crops, but the wood will need oiling or preserving, unlike aluminium which will take care of itself. Buying a greenhouse might sound like a big investment, but the return you can get in terms of plants, crops and sheer satisfaction will make it well worth the money.

Any greenhouse must have good ventilation, as they can get very hot in the summer and this can kill your precious plants. Think about how much staging (built-in benches for holding pots) you want and how much bare border soil you need if you are intending to grow melons, aubergines, greenhouse cucumbers and indoor tomatoes, which will stay in the greenhouse all summer.

POLYTUNNELS

If you have bags of land to hide away an ugly structure and want to grow lots of produce, then consider buying a polytunnel. The one I had on my last allotment, which was 4.3 x 8.6m (14 x 28ft), was large enough to house all the summer and winter crops, plus a large water butt and an old picnic table for family meals on rainy days. I loved my polytunnel because it grew strong and healthy plants, thanks to the even light levels inside.

A small 4.3m (14ft) polytunnel is comparable in price to a small greenhouse, or you could look out for a second-hand one – buy the doors and hoops, but expect to buy new plastic as old ones tend to be ripped or dirty. Ideally try to get a polytunnel with double doors at either end for good ventilation and adhesive gutters for collecting water off the side, as well as insulation tape to cover the hoops to prevent heat damage to the plastic where it touches the metal frame. You can get different types of plastic, but always choose one with at least a four-year guarantee. I prefer the thermal, anti-fog type that is opaque (more private) and holds in the heat better than clear plastic, which will allow you to extend the growing seasons either side of summer. Anti-fog plastic also reduces condensation, which helps avoid conditions that promote grey mould and mildews (see p.194).

Polytunnels can be fiddly to put up. You will need at least one extra pair of hands to help, a day to put up the hoops and another to cover it with plastic. Putting up a polytunnel also needs to be done when it is sunny, as it makes the plastic more pliable and allows you to stretch it drum-tight over the hoops.

tip

Before you erect your polytunnel, make sure the ground is weed-free, both inside and in the area around the proposed perimeter, as it is very difficult to weed up against the plastic.

RECLAIMED GREENHOUSES

My greenhouse was originally designed and made as a centrepiece for a show garden at BBC 'Gardeners' World Live'. For weeks I collected unwanted window frames and sourced salvage timber to make up the sides and roof. After the show I took it down and brought it back to replace my old greenhouse.

Making your own greenhouse is a bit like designing your dream kitchen, packed with features to make life easier and to make you happy when you're in it. Mine is made from reclaimed Douglas fir and pitch pine, along with salvaged window frames, sunk into the ground to create raised beds that trap heat in winter and retain moisture in summer.

The white-painted back wall is clad with timber to create a feeling of privacy and also to bounce light back onto the raised beds. The floor is decked with recycled ceiling joists. It's easy to sweep clean and, because it traps moisture between the cracks, it is also good for damping down in the summer. The roof is partly clad in lead to create a home for cliff-top plants, such as stonecrop and lampranthus, while the round windows have no particular function apart from letting in light, but they do make it feel more magical inside.

tip

Guttering kits are available for aluminium greenhouses to harvest rainwater, but it is also quite easy to make your own from recycled or new gutters and downpipes. Guttering that is 8cm (3in) wide is ideal and should be installed just as you would house guttering by clipping it onto brackets positioned just below the roof panes. Unlike house guttering, however, because the gutter length on a greenhouse is so short it does not need to slope towards the downpipe in order to drain, so just make sure it is level and direct the downpipe into a water butt.

SITING AND ERECTING YOUR GREENHOUSE

Position your greenhouse in as much sun as possible. Often, in an established garden, existing features determine the angle it faces, but if you have the choice, angle the ridge north to south for growing vegetables (so the sun illuminates both sides) and east to west for flowers. Flowers grown on the north side of the greenhouse will then turn to face into the greenhouse so that you can enjoy them better.

When it comes to putting up your greenhouse think of it as a two-person, two-stage job. New greenhouses come with instructions, but if you want to include a solid path, like the brick path on p.36, it is best to lay it first.

GREENHOUSE ESSENTIALS

Whatever type of greenhouse you choose you will need to have this basic kit:

■ **Staging.** These are usually slatted wood or aluminium benches, but you can make your own using concrete blocks as supports and timber planks for the top.

■ **Guttering and a water butt.** To catch rainwater from the roof. (see tip, opposite).

■ **Ventilation.** Some greenhouses come with automatic vent openers that respond to a rise in temperature, others will need to be opened manually when the temperatures rise. A 2 x 2.5m (6 x 8ft) greenhouse will need at least two roof vents.

■ **Watering can.** With a rose to disperse water for gentle watering of seedlings.

■ **Shading.** The simplest type of shading is a distemper-like paint that you apply in early summer to keep the inside cooler and rub off in the autumn when light levels drop. It doesn't have to look ugly; try painting it on in stripes and it can look quite funky! Ready-made rolls of cut willow, that are sold as screens at garden centres and online, can also be used as blinds by securing it to the ridge on the outside and draping it over the roof panes. If you have the money to spare, custom-made blinds are also available, but fleece is just as good and far cheaper.

■ **Heaters.** These are essential if you want to grow tropical exotics, such as orchids, or overwinter tender cuttings, such as pelargonium. Electric or gas heaters, controlled by a thermostat, are available from garden centres or specialist suppliers and give you greater temperature control than paraffin heaters. Although paraffin heaters are often the cheapest to buy, running them can be expensive and unpleasantly smoky.

Aluminium-framed greenhouses don't need foundations and therefore can be placed straight onto level ground. To stop them from blowing away they are bolted to metal stakes that are driven into the ground. If you are lucky enough to inherit a greenhouse from a friend, or you manage to find a second-hand one, be sure to take lots of pictures before you dismantle it. Make sure you photograph the joins and how the windows and doors fit into the structure, because once it is taken apart, a greenhouse can be more difficult than a Rubik's Cube to get back together again.

Timber greenhouses usually sit on a low wall made of brick or concrete blocks that are rendered to make them more ornamental. Always put a layer of damp-proof membrane between the top of the bricks or blocks and the timber to prevent moisture from soaking up and rotting the wood.

tip

Bring new bags of compost into the greenhouse before sowing to warm up and give seeds a head start.

Gutter. Collect water from the roof of your greenhouse and direct it into a water butt.

Height. If you are building your own, make it tall. The greater the volume of air, the less the air temperature fluctuates so plants will thrive. By sinking a path down the middle of the greenhouse, and retaining the soil on either side, you can improve the volume of any greenhouse. Sink the greenhouse into a slope if possible, as this also creates extra head-height for training cucumbers along the ridge.

Dip tank. A metal tank, such as an old water tank, makes filling watering cans much easier. If you have space, keep the tank inside the greenhouse as it acts like a heat sink and will reduce the risk of frost in the winter.

Wires and supports. Fix permanent wires along the ridge to save time and make training plants such as cucumbers and tomatoes easier.

Shelves. Shelves can provide extra space for pots when the greenhouse gets busy in the spring. When the plants move out into the garden, remove the shelves to make room for tall crops such as tomatoes and cucumbers.

Power socket. A good investment; a waterproof electric socket will allow you to have a heated propagating bench, run greenhouse heaters and grow lamps, and light your greenhouse.

Raised beds. I sow early salads, such as spinach and rocket, in late winter, replace them with coriander and basil as the weather warms up and follow with tender summer crops.

Ventilation. Doors and windows that open on all sides of the greenhouse create a through draft that cools in the summer and blows away fungal spores in the spring and autumn. Some come with automatic vent openers that respond to a rise in temperature, or you can buy and install them yourself later.

Portable potting bench. In spring the potting bench is best inside the greenhouse, but it can be moved outside in the summer to free up space for plants such as tomatoes. A customized bench means you can have it at a comfortable height, alternatively you can prop up bought benches on cheap concrete blocks.

Max–min thermometer. This records the current temperature, as well as how hot and cold your greenhouse gets in a 24-hour period.

Raised beds. I used concrete blocks and rendered them, alternatively use stacked chunky timbers screwed to tree stakes that are hammered in the ground to keep them in place. This type of bed brings plants up to eye-level and makes it easier to spot and deal with pests before they become a problem. The soil in raised beds also drains and warms up more quickly.

MAKE A FLEECE TUNNEL

If you don't have a greenhouse, or it's packed to the gunnels with overwintering plants and cuttings, you can quite easily make a fleece tunnel for outdoor sowings of salads for early spring (February) and late autumn (October). It will protect them from the worst of the weather and reward you with out-of-season crops. It is constructed like a single-hoop tent by bending a 2m (6ft) stick into a curve, draping a rectangle of horticultural fleece over it and pinning down each corner with a brick. Any type of stick will do as long as it is bendy. Use more hoops and fleece to make a longer tunnel and cover larger areas.

COLDFRAMES AND MINI GREENHOUSES

If you have a limited space or budget then a coldframe or mini greenhouse can be a better choice than a full-sized greenhouse, especially if the majority of your sowing is in spring. A coldframe is a glass-topped box that provides some shelter from the elements. It can be positioned just outside the back door of your house and is perfect if all you want to do is sow a few annuals and vegetables, such as marigolds and French beans.

Similarly, mini greenhouses can be positioned against the back of the house and take up very little space, while still having enough room for trays of seed-sown vegetables, hardy annuals and perennials.

An old sash window from a reclaim yard or skip makes a good roof for a homemade coldframe. Either use timber planks to make the sides, or stacks of bricks. Make sure it is in a sunny position and slant the glass towards the sun so it catches the maximum amount of light and sheds the rain.

tip

Pot up bulbs such as miniature daffodils and tulips and keep them in the greenhouse. They will come into flower earlier than those outdoors and make good gap fillers in your borders.

MAKE A PROPAGATION BENCH

Every greenhouse I have ever had, even my first one, has had a propagation bench. Essentially this is a rectangular wooden tray, about 60cm x 1.2m (2 x 4ft) that sits on top of a bench and is used for propagating seeds and cuttings. To encourage seeds to germinate and cuttings to root, it is heated. While you can buy electric propagators that provide bottom heat, they tend to be small so I prefer to make my own by lining the tray with plastic and pouring a mixture of sand and compost over soil-warming cables.

The cables can raise the temperature of the sand-compost mix by around 10–13°C (50–55°F) above the ambient greenhouse temperature, thereby warming the pots of seeds and cuttings. It makes a huge difference to my success rate, especially with tender crops such as chilli peppers and tomatoes that need heat to sprout, and means that they come into production weeks earlier than ones grown on a cold bench.

You can also root cuttings straight into the sand-compost mix, particularly basal cuttings, such as dahlias and pelargonium, succulents, woody herbs and all those winter-insurance cuttings, such as penstemon and osteospermum.

Your greenhouse will need to have an electric socket and a sturdy base for the propagation bench to sit on. Soil-warming cables come as kits and many include a thermostat, which allows you to control the temperature. Kits come with different lengths of cable for making large and small propagating benches, but for the box shown below you will need a 6m (20ft) cable.

1 Corner battens in corners for extra strength

2 Timber box, 120 x 60cm (4 x 2ft) made with 15cm (6in) planks

3 Plastic liner made from old compost bags to protect the wood

4 50/50 washed sand and seed compost mix filled to the top of the box

5 Heated cables set out with 8–10cm (3–4in) spaces between them

6 Thermostat sits above the cables

7 Hole halfway up the side at one end for the thermostat

8 Cable to a waterproof power point

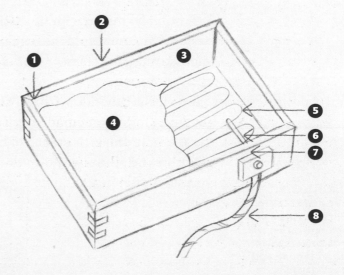

GREENHOUSE TECHNIQUES

The name of the game with greenhouses is to create an even growing environment where the temperature does not plummet or soar, and where plants neither grow in the shade nor are scorched by the sun. For this reason doors and windows are more than just entry and exit points for people, they are also the mechanisms by which temperature, air moisture and light levels can be controlled. These are all things that plants rely on to thrive.

■ **Heating.** I think the best heaters are thermostatically controlled, electric fan heaters that are designed to hang from the roof-ridge and can be fairly cheap to buy. Because warm air rises, the fan circulates it back down to the plants, and by keeping the air moving the risk of fungal infection, which is exacerbated by stagnant air, is reduced. Choose a heater with a fan that runs independently of the heating element so you can use it to circulate air without heating it.

■ **Venting.** A greenhouse in summer can be as hot as a desert, producing conditions that can kill plants, so opening windows and doors are essential to allow air circulation to cool things down. In spring and autumn, open the doors on warm days, but close the greenhouse in the late afternoon or early evening to hold in the heat at night. In summer, doors and windows can be left open all the time, unless gale-force winds are forecast or, of course, you have a collection of heat-loving plants. In the winter, keep the greenhouse shut up on days when the temperature drops below 8°C (46°F). You can take your chances on those few and far-between sunny winter days, when the temperature rises above 8°C (46°F), to open the doors and clear the greenhouse of fungal spores.

■ **Shading.** Tomatoes prefer to be shaded, but bell and chilli peppers can take hotter temperatures and the leaves won't scorch. Pin fleece or netting up to the glass on the sunny side, or paint special greenhouse paint onto the glass in early summer.

■ **Bubble wrapping.** Pinning bubble wrap to the inside frame of your greenhouse, or part of it if you have a large greenhouse, slows the speed at which the temperature falls on cold nights and saves money on heating. I prefer the big bubble wrap as it looks neater and being thicker has a longer working life.

■ **Damping down.** When it is hot and dry, hosing down the paths and soil in a greenhouse will instantly cool it down and fill the air with much-needed moisture, which means your plants will transpire (lose moisture) less from their foliage.

GREAT GREENHOUSE CROPS

Greenhouses serve three main purposes. Firstly, they give your plants a head start and allow you to sow vegetables earlier, thus giving you an earlier crop. Secondly, they extend the season by providing a home for late-sown crops, such as salads, so they can keep cropping into autumn and winter. Finally, they provide a summer home for plants that prefer hotter and more sheltered conditions in order to crop, such as chilli peppers and aubergines.

You can grow traditional outdoor crops, such as potatoes and sweet corn, in the greenhouse to produce out-of-season crops. Warmer conditions can also make plant growth softer, which makes traditionally tough vegetables like Tuscan kale and spring cabbage more succulent.

tip

If you don't have a heated greenhouse propagator, start plants off indoors on a warm, bright windowsill and grow them on in an airy, but frost-free, place, such as a closed porch.

AUBERGINES

You might not get big crops of aubergines, but they are worth growing and will be a creamy revelation compared to the cardboard types you can buy in shops. Sow, grow and feed them just like tomatoes. They are harder to grow from seed and need more heat to grow on from seedlings, but like tomatoes you can also buy them ready grown from garden centres. Aubergines relish slightly warmer and more humid growing conditions than tomatoes, so are a particularly good crop for a polytunnel.

You will need to stake them to a cane, but take care as they have quite vicious thorns (particularly the white and red ones). Aubergines do not crop heavily, but to encourage crop production create branched plants by pinching out the growing tip when the plant is 25cm (10in) tall. Mist them daily once the flowers appear to help them set fruit and prevent problems with red spider mite, which hates damp conditions.

The traditional black aubergines are ready to harvest when they are plump and glossy purple. It is less easy to tell when other varieties are ripe so you will have to rely on intuition – keep a beady eye on their development and pick them when they stop swelling, but before the skin starts to crack.

TOMATOES

Although tomatoes can be grown outside, they are more reliable if they are grown in the greenhouse, where they are protected from the scourge of wet summers and a fungal disease called blight. Although they are not quite as flavourful as outdoor tomatoes, greenhouse plants crop earlier and continue for longer. Any tomato variety can be grown under cover.

Sow a dozen or so seeds in a 10cm (4in) pot in February or March and put them in a propagator set to 21°C (70°F), alternatively, look for ready-grown young plants in garden centres. Prick out seedlings into individual 8cm (3in) pots and grow them on under cover, ideally on a propagator bench. When temperatures warm up, around late April, either plant them out in the greenhouse border or pot them up into larger 12cm (5in) pots and grow on.

To save space I grow cordon varieties that can be pruned to produce a single, long stem. As they grow, I tie the stem onto twine that is tied to the roof of the greenhouse. If you pinch out any side shoots that grow in the fork where the leaves meet the stem it will focus the plant's energy into tomato production and stop the plants becoming congested. Feed once every two weeks with a liquid high-potash fertilizer as soon as pea-sized fruits appear.

CUCUMBERS

Of the greenhouse cucumber varieties, my favourite are those with short fruit, such as 'Passandra' and 'Fadia'. They taste delicious and lend themselves to training along the roof ridge, thereby saving space and helping to shade the greenhouse. What's more, you won't bang your head on the swelling fruits.

Opt for all-female varieties; they are pricier, but it prevents pollination between male and female flowers that results in bitter-tasting cucumbers. If you decide not to grow an all-female variety, pinch out male flowers as they grow – they can be identified by the lack of the embryonic fruit behind the tubular yellow flowers.

Sow a single seed, in late March or April, on its side in a 8cm (3in) pot in a propagator set to 21°C (70°F). Plant out in greenhouse borders, or 30cm (12in) containers, in May when

tip

You can also use growbags in the greenhouse. Maximize their depth by cutting them in half and standing them on end to make two containers. Before slicing through the plastic, wrap packing tape around the bag to create a solid rim so bags won't tear when they are moved.

LEFT: One of my favourite ways to spend a rainy summer day – training the stems of tomatoes bathed in the appetite-whetting, resin-scent of the foliage. Bring on the basil and mozzarella!

the plants have three good leaves. Some gardeners train the stems to canes, but I use twine with one end wrapped around the stem and the other lashed to, and along, the greenhouse roof. This also serves the purpose of providing living greenhouse shading.

Once the seedlings get going and the weather warms up, keep humidity levels up by damping down when it's hot and placing a bucket of water at the base of the plants. Although cucumbers like moist soil, it's best not to wet the leaves as this can encourage fungal infections. Pick regularly when they are over 15cm (6in) long, to keep new cucumbers coming, and remember to feed the plants about every two weeks with a high-potash tomato-type fertilizer.

BELL PEPPERS AND CHILLIES

Peppers also grow like tomatoes, but they prefer drier and brighter conditions so I never put them in the shadier parts of the greenhouse. Both bell peppers and fiendishly fiery chillies are easy to produce from seed. Grow them as you would for tomatoes, but once the plant gets to around 30cm (12in),

tip

Cut a cucumber in half, leaving one end still attached to the stem. A new skin will grow over the wound. Save half the cucumber for later – one to remember in years when crops are scarce!

African marigolds make good playmates for bell peppers as their flowers attract whitefly-eating hoverflies. Besides, I love their oily scent in a hot greenhouse.

pinch out the top 2cm ($^3/_4$in) of the stem. This will make them bushier, which means they will bear more peppers. Feed every week with a high-potash tomato fertilizer and keep colonies of whitefly and spider mites down by misting plants with water and damping down the floor.

To maximize bell pepper crops, pick your first peppers when they are still green, as the first ones will stop others from developing if you leave them on the plant for too long. All peppers ripen from green (or occasionally black) through to red, and although green chillies are meant to be milder I think the red ones have a much fuller taste to them. Chillies are a great autumn crop because you can dry them on the greenhouse bench and they keep for kitchen use right through winter.

tip

The shoulders of chilli peppers are hotter than the tip. This often fools the unwary, and then wham! Always wash your hands after handling and cutting up peppers, as the juice can really sting your eyes (and other places, I'm told!).

MELONS

Just the scent of a melon swelling in your greenhouse makes it worth trying, even though they are not easy to grow. I've had my best luck with cantaloupe melons grown in a polytunnel, as they like humidity. The key to success is not to be greedy; only allow four or five fruits to develop at most, otherwise you will end up with lots of very small fruit.

Sow in late April, as you would a cucumber. When the seeds germinate, grow the plants on in a heated greenhouse, in a minimum temperature of 12°C (54°F), until they have three leaves, then plant out into the greenhouse border. Melon plants are hungry, so improve the soil with compost first.

As the plants grow, train the shoots up canes or string, and mulch with more compost. Melons like humidity so water them in the heat of the day, but be careful not to overdo it as they will quickly rot if soil stays sodden. Once the yellow, trumpet-like flowers appear, pollinate them by hand by removing the male flowers and brushing them against the female flowers (the female has a baby melon behind the flower).

When the growing tip reaches the roof of the greenhouse pinch it out to encourage fruit-bearing side shoots. When melons appear, count two leaves beyond each one and snip off any further leaves to direct the plant's energy into the fruit. Once the fruit starts to swell, feed the plant every two weeks with a liquid high-potash fertilizer and make sure it is shaded from the sun.

The melons are ready when they fill the air with a sweet, sticky fragrance and small cracks appear where the stalk joins the fruit. Don't leave them for too long before picking though, which is what I once did. Showing off my first, great melon-growing success I left the fruit on for too long and they fermented and went off.

BRASSICAS

Spring cabbage is a great crop for forcing in a polytunnel border in late summer and early autumn to provide fresh succulent greens throughout winter. Sow it directly into borders, broadcasting in blocks for leafy greens that will cut-and-come-again. You can also sow turnips, kohl rabi and calabrese in the same way. I use them shredded and fried in butter and as a useful green filler for tomato-based sauces and winter casseroles.

SALAD LEAVES AND MICRO-GREENS

You don't need to heat your greenhouse to have fresh crops of salad leaves in spring and autumn. Sow Chinese cabbage and pak choi in late summer or early autumn and it will crop right up to Christmas. Oriental greens (mizuna and mustard) will hang on right through winter if they are sown at the same time. I do mine in my raised beds, but you can also grow them in trays on a greenhouse bench or under fleece tunnels at the allotment. Growing micro-greens produces a fast crop – less than a week in the summer – and, if your greenhouse is heated, they will grow right through winter. Micro-greens are seed leaves or very young plants that can be eaten stem and all for their intense flavour and high natural vitamin and mineral content. Many vegetable seedlings are edible, but some should be avoided, such as tomatoes, aubergines, peppers, potatoes and rhubarb. As a rule, if you can eat the leaves of the adult plant, you can eat the seedlings too.

Micro-greens are easy to grow in compost-filled seed trays or old fruit boxes lined with newspaper. Spacing seeds 0.5–1cm (¼–½in) apart. Keep them in a coldframe or greenhouse and cut like cress when the seedlings are 5–10cm (2–4in) tall.

RIGHT: Salad leaves are ideal for the impatient. You can eat them as spicy seedlings, baby leaves or wait until the leaves are big and crisp.

BEST MICRO-GREENS

- **Lovage.** The leaves sprout in ten to 14 days and taste like fresh celery. Great for potato soups.

- **Red cabbage.** This has a 'long' flavour that starts off sweet and ends in a peppery bite. A handful of these purple stems will transform a humble egg sandwich into something that even Gordon Ramsay would rate.

- **Red mustard.** Normally a coarse and spicy leaf that has the look of leather, but when it is eaten as a seedling it tastes far more delicate.

- **Mizuna.** A refreshing, pallet-cleansing taste that is quite different from the spicy mature leaf.

- **Fennel.** Sweet aniseed taste that goes fabulously with fish.

- **Peas.** The leaves taste just like freshly podded peas and can be produced well out of season.

- **Orache.** A micro-green with a sorrel-like flavour.

GREENHOUSE PESTS AND DISEASES

If there is a downside to greenhouses it is that the warm and sheltered conditions make a good breeding ground for pests such as whitefly and red spider mites. If you have had a bad infestation it's often a good idea to give the whole greenhouse a good scrub when the growing season has finished. A jet washer is best for getting into the nooks and crannies where eggs and insects hide, as well as getting algae off the windows. If you don't have one, you can hire them or borrow one from a car-proud friend.

The good news is that many pests, including whitefly, red spider mite and mealy bugs, have natural predators that also thrive in greenhouse conditions (see p.225). Be aware, however, that if you introduce biological controls into your greenhouse you cannot use chemical solutions. There are also environmentally friendly sprays, such as insecticidal soaps and mineral-based plant invigorators (see p.223). Insecticidal soaps work by gumming up pests and stopping them feeding. Plant invigorators not only feed the plant, but also 'glue' pests such as whitefly in one place so they can't breed, feed or live for very long.

Here are some of the major pests and diseases that you might encounter in your greenhouse:

APHIDS

The first sign of aphids is distorted leaves then, when the plant gets infested, it becomes sticky and a black mould appears on the surface of the foliage. Aphids are tiny, apple green, grey, fawn or black insects with cricket-like legs and nodding antennae. They can attack at any time of year and numbers build up fast so you need to act quickly. Patrol your plants regularly and rub or hose off any infestations, normally gathered round the soft tips.

Plant invigorators work well and if you have large plants that are difficult to reach then bio control is also a good option – *Aphidius* or *Aphidoletes* are naturally-occurring parasites and midges that work in temperatures above 18°C (64°F); lacewing larvae are active in temperatures above 10°C (50°F). Professional growers often use tobacco plants as a kind of sacrificial crop, as the aphids get stuck to the sticky flower stems.

WHITEFLY

Whitefly look like specks of white wood ash on plant foliage. Leaves feels sticky and when you touch them the air suddenly comes alive with a plume of white flies. These tiny creatures are resistant to pretty much every chemical on the amateur market, and can survive all year round if your greenhouse is warm.

Because they suck the plant's sap and breed like wildfire, whitefly can ruin every plant in the greenhouse within the space of a week, so they need to be dealt with. Again, I use plant invigorators, which are especially good with peppers, but if you have a larger or permanently heated greenhouse or conservatory (above 18°C/64°F) then it is a good idea to use *Encasia formosa* (a parasitic wasp) that can be bought by mail order in the form of eggs. They are so tiny that you won't notice them, but they can impact heavily on whitefly numbers.

RED SPIDER MITE

Plants take on a grey, anaemic look, often with a yellow mottling, when red spider mite is about, and in very bad attacks you will notice webbing between the stems and leaves. They love aubergines and cucumbers and tend to go for plants in poor health. Watering properly, keeping the greenhouse damped down and misting leaves (not the leaves of cucumbers) is a good preventative, as red spider mites love hot, dry conditions.

In warm greenhouses, over 18°C (64°F), biological control can be used in the form of a predatory mite called *Phytoseiulus persimilis*. Plant invigorators on aubergines and cucumbers are also good as a preventative.

POWDERY MILDEW

This fungal disease looks like a dusting of talc, starting off as spots of white or jaundiced yellow, and gradually joining up to cover the leaf surface. It attacks plants when they are dry at the roots and air circulation is poor, so keep the greenhouse well ventilated on hot days and keep your plants watered. A sulphur-based fungicide can check its spread, but once leaves are damaged they have to be pruned off as the fungus causes black scars. The trimmings can go on the compost heap without re-infecting your plants. Plant invigorators also work well as a preventative.

GREY MOULD

This is the same white, fluffy mould that appears in your fruit bowl if you leave fruit to fester. It is caused by damp, humid conditions and spreads from dead material to living. Keep plants free of dead stems, fallen leaves and old fruit to prevent its spread, and open the doors on warm days in winter to blow away spores. Prunings can go on the compost heap without risk of re-infection.

DAMPING OFF

This fungal disease, which spreads in cool, wet, muggy conditions, can suddenly attack and kill your otherwise healthy seedlings. To combat it, keep pots clean and never use unsterilized garden soil in your potting mixes or irrigate your seedlings with water from the water butt. You can't save infected seedlings, so I'm afraid you will have to start over again

CATERPILLAR

Obvious signs of caterpillar attack are distorted, holey or webbed leaves. The problem peaks when the eggs hatch in early summer and often again in autumn. If you don't garden organically there are chemical insecticides, but you won't be able to use it in conjunction with any of the other biological controls I mention here (see p.225). Picking caterpillars off by hand is the most virtuous way and most plants that are robust enough to take a quick shake will bring caterpillars tumbling to the bench, where they can be escorted off the premises and to a bird table.

MEALY BUG

These grey, lentil-shaped, slightly fluffy creatures are more repugnant than they sound. Found on the underside of leaves and in the joins between leaf and stem, they adore cacti and succulents, but will also attack permanent plants such as jasmine and grapevines. They attack in autumn when temperatures are dropping, but the biological control (*cryptolaemus*) that controls them needs constant temperatures of 20°C (68°F) and above, so it only works in highly-heated greenhouses. They cover themselves and their eggs in a special wax that makes them immune to sprays, but plant invigorators will remove the wax and kill them.

As the great bard might have said if he'd been a gardener: 'Pests come not as single spies, they come in battalions'. Here are the classic signs of red spider mite on an aubergine leaf, with a bit of nibbling by a slug.

LAWNS

There is plenty of good advice around about lawn care that can give the impression that creating a lawn is a lot of hard work, but you don't have to make a religion out of it. Few people care about flowering daisies in their lawn – they are really only a problem if drought or trampling kids kill them off and leave bare patches. When it comes to lawns it is often worth remembering the advice of the late, great plantsman Christopher Lloyd. When asked what he did when his lawn went brown in the summer, he replied: 'I look at something else'.

Even if there are a few weeds, a neat and tidy lawn with a clearly defined edge can make a garden look 'done'. Unlike paving and gravel, lawns absorb heat from the sun and create a cooler atmosphere in the garden. This is better for plants and reduces the stifling heat of summer in urban areas. Not to mention the obvious fact that they are far more comfortable for picnics. Then again, you might want the English stripy lawn, as soft and spongy as Axminster under your bare feet, or the green Grade-1 crop of a bowling green, made from grasses as fine as hair. A lawn like this doesn't come easy, but, as with any collection of plant species you cherish, it is worth it. Think of a lawn less as a surface to walk, rest and play on, and more as a pet.

Lawns also do a great service to the environment by providing a 'safe green zone' for birds to feed, where they can spot cats coming, and by improving drainage in built-up areas, allowing rainwater to sink into the ground rather than overwhelm the drains and road gutters. They are also a source of free homemade compost, as lawn clippings make fabulous compost-box fillers and the nitrogen-rich clippings are a superb bulky material to add to the compost heap. Lawns are also great custodians, guarding the health of the soil beneath it, unlike gravel toppings that tend to allow nutrients to be washed away.

LOVELY LAWNS WITHOUT THE LEGWORK

■ Keep the lawn longer in summer, around 5–10cm (2–4in). This will make it far less susceptible to drought, and shady lawns will also benefit as it will make them less prone to moss and bare patches.

■ Keep your mower well maintained and the blades sharp. Cutting a lawn with blunt blades bruises the grass and makes fungal infection more likely.

■ Cut your lawn regularly, at least once a week in the summer and once every two weeks in the spring, autumn and warm winters. Regular trimming encourages the roots to spread, which fills gaps and blocks out weeds.

■ Never cut grass down by more than half its height as this will weaken subsequent growth and make the lawn more susceptible to drought and vulnerable to invading weeds. If your lawn is long, reduce the height gradually over a few weeks.

■ If you walk over your lawn regularly, set stepping-stones into it or sprinkle 1cm ($\frac{1}{2}$in) of horticultural grit into the area that is most used to reduce compaction of the soil.

WHAT'S IN A LAWN?

Lawns are made up of several species of grass mixed into a tapestry to create a specific lawn. Of the most common grasses, some are spreading and keel-shaped, like bents; broad-leafed like rye grass; and narrow like the fescues that give a fine appear-ance to a lawn. Rye grass forms the body of a lawn, the bents stop it looking threadbare, and the fescues make it soft to touch.

One of the best and most recent developments in lawn species is RTF (Rhizomatous Tall Fescue), a deep-rooted, relatively coarse grass that is able to withstand long periods of drought. I was impressed by its tolerance for growing and staying green under a trampoline, where it was shady and dry. It is available as grass or turf and, although it is not as fine looking as rye grass, it is perfect for shady city gardens where grass usually struggles.

PREPARING FOR A NEW LAWN

Whether you choose to sow seed or lay rolls of turf, preparation is key. If you have a large garden, rotavate or fork over the

tip

When you are designing your garden, decide on the shape of your lawn first and use it to plan the shape of your borders, not the other way around. Take a good long look out of a top window of your house to determine the best shape for your garden. Think of the impact a rug has in a room – you should notice the shape of the rug and not the space around it. Even if it is only a tiny lawn, it should be at least big enough to lie down and sunbathe on or to spread out the picnic blanket!

ground first, to break up the soil. Then use a fork, followed by a rake, to level the area, removing any large stones and roots that are near the surface. Once the area is roughly level, tread down the soil with your feet.

Apply a bonemeal dressing and then rake the area flat again. The way to achieve a perfectly level lawn is to rake first one way, and then at 90 degrees to the first raking – this will fill in any small gaps. It is worth taking your time doing this, as you will be stuck with any hollows or bumps once the grass grows. If you are replacing scrubby, old grass dig it out in small amounts, but if it is a larger or mossy area lift it as you would turf (see p.25) as it will be hard to get it level otherwise.

LAYING TURF

Laying turf will radically transform your garden in just a few hours, and is the closest thing to a TV makeover for your garden that you are ever likely to get. Although turf is more expensive than seed, it gives you a useable lawn, albeit with care, in just a few weeks, while seed takes up to six months to establish. You can also lay turf at any time of the year, provided the ground isn't waterlogged or frozen.

With turf you get what you pay for. The cheapest type is meadow grass, which gives a shaggy, often weedy, lawn of variable quality, and I've seen some terrible examples. At the opposite end of the spectrum is sea-washed turf – a fine, expensive lawn that doesn't like being walked on too much and needs very regular care and mowing. If you want a good-quality standard turf that will grow into a perfectly presentable lawn I would suggest a fine rye grass mix (containing fescues and bents) or one of the new breeds of RTFs that have very deep roots and can survive neglect and dry conditions.

Buy your turf from a specialist supplier, who can give you details about its quality and whether your growing conditions are suitable for the grass mix it contains. Turf is sold in units of 1m (40in), which are usually 50cm (20in) wide and 2m (6ft) long and supplied in rolls. When it arrives check it is not yellow and dry, a bad sign as it should have been lifted only the day before or even the day it's laid so the grass doesn't take too much of a check to its growth.

It is always best to lay turf on the day it arrives, while it is still fresh. If you can't do this then make sure you unroll it to expose grass to the light, or it will go yellow. I always do the outside of the lawn first, so there are no small, prone-to-drying-out pieces left around the edge. I lay it a few inches wider than I want the lawn to be so I can trim it up neatly later. I then lay the rest of the area with staggered joints in a brickwork pattern, using a bread knife to cut the turf to size. I always work off a wooden plank rather than treading on the grass so as not to damage the turf.

Pat the turf into place, making sure the joints are nice and tight. When you get to the end of a row don't try to judge the size of the turf by eye, instead lay the turf down and cut it to fit first. Once all the turf has been laid, keep it well watered until the turf starts to grow or the individual turfs will dry out and shrink, leaving gaps that won't knit together. Cut it on the mower's highest blade setting once the turf gets to about 5cm (2in) tall. You can start light use – walking and cutting – from about two weeks after laying.

SOWING A LAWN FROM SEED

Seed is more economical than turf and you can buy grass seed to suit your site – fine turf mixes, resilient family lawns, shade-tolerant, and so on. On the downside, you are more restricted with when you can sow your lawn. The ideal time is early autumn when the soil is still warm from the summer, but moist; don't sow in periods of hot, dry weather. Sowing in spring is possible, but in my experience less reliable and more work, as you need to do lots of watering if the weather suddenly heats up.

All grass seed comes with a sowing rate that is measured in grams per square metre. To make it easier, I measure out enough seed for $1m^2$ on a set of kitchen scales, put it in a plastic cup and mark the line with a pen so I know how much to measure out for the rest of the area. Similarly, to work out the size of your area, mark out $1m^2$ with canes and then guess the rest by eye.

Scatter the seed from your hand rather than from the measuring cup. To make sure I get even coverage, I sow first across the lawn

tip

Shake the packet of grass seed regularly during sowing to ensure species with smaller seed are evenly distributed throughout the mix, rather than falling to the bottom.

and then up and down over each metre, working backwards so you don't walk over newly sown areas. If you are doing a really large area, it is a good idea to check every so often that you are still sowing the right amount of grass in the right-size area.

After sowing keep off the lawn and don't water it immediately or it will wash the seeds about and clump them together. Birds can be a problem so you might have to net the area to keep them off – make sure it is pegged down well so they don't get trapped underneath it. Once the seeds have sprouted, water when the soil surface dries out. Grass can be up within a fortnight but will take up to five months to thicken out. Give the lawn its first cut, with the mower blade on its highest setting, when it is about 5cm (2in) tall and start to fertilize the following spring. Grass seed lasts for ages when stored in an airtight box somewhere dry and cool, so it's a good idea to keep any leftover seed to fill in any bare patches.

Make sowing a lawn a faster job by first weighing out the amount of grass seed you'll need per square metre and mark the level on the side of a clear plastic cup.

 tip

Grass seed is ideal for over-sowing threadbare lawns and bare patches after scarifying (see p.204). Sow it at half the rate recommended on the packet.

BASIC LAWN CARE

Time was when the lawn was a source of pride, the doormat in front of the 'Englishman's castle', but these days most people take a more relaxed approach to it. You might not have an intensive programme of lawn care worked out in the diary, but if your lawn starts to look a bit lacklustre it is amazing how quickly it responds to attention. A bit of spiking to aerate the trampled goalmouth of your son's football posts can work wonders to get the grass growing again, while raking out the dead grass can turn a thin, threadbare lawn back into a dense, soft, green picnic blanket.

FEEDING

In March, when the grass starts to grow, buy a balanced lawn fertilizer. Don't overdo it, and avoid the borders, otherwise your garden will look like you have run amok with a flame-thrower. If you have a large lawn, invest in a wheeled lawn feeder for a faster and more accurate job.

Try and apply fertilizer when rain is forecast, so that it gets washed down to the roots of the grass and to stop it from burning the leaf blades; water the fertilizer in well yourself if it doesn't rain. Results will begin to show within the week, as your grass looks visibly lusher and greener. Feed again in midsummer, but don't feed newly sown grass or recently laid turf as it will scorch and turn brown.

A good organic alternative to chemical lawn fertilizers is liquid seaweed, which you apply once a month from spring through to late summer. It acts as a good preventative to problems and a boost for grass growing in difficult areas, such as under trees where the soil often lacks nutrients. Seaweed is a biostimulant that increases the vigour of plants when conditions are less than ideal, thereby warding off weeds and moss that tend to invade grass that's growing poorly.

WATERING

Watering is essential for a young, establishing lawn, as a dry spell can kill both turf and grass growing from seed. Always water young lawns thoroughly. In hot weather, if it doesn't rain for a few days, get out the hose or sprinkler and leave it on for a couple of hours in the evening, so that less water is wasted through evaporation.

Established lawns also need watering in prolonged periods of summer drought if you want them to stay green. If left un-watered they will survive and green up again with the autumn rains, but some of the finer grass species may be killed, which will reduce the quality of your lawn and the dead patches will need re-sowing. Longer grass goes brown less quickly because the plants are less stressed from being cut back, so a good trick is to raise your mower blades in a dry summer.

If you think watering is an unnecessary expense to your purse and the environment, then choose an RTF. Although it is coarser, its deeper roots allow it to stay green and survive drought for longer.

WEEDING

Feeding and regular mowing is far better and more environmentally-friendly as a weed-preventative – particularly if you have pets and young children – than using weedkillers that are expensive and ultimately don't address the reason that the weeds are there, which is poor grass health.

The worst weeds, in my view, are plantains and dandelions as they have spreading leaves that can smother large areas of lawn. Their size, though, is their downfall, as they are easy to trowel out, roots and all. Yellow medick, buttercups and clover can also spread quickly through a lawn, so raking before you mow can help to lift them up into the blades of the mower, thereby weakening and killing them off over time.

EDGING

Edging is done with a pair of long-handled shears and defines the edge of your lawn, stops the grass growing into borders and instantly neatens up your garden. Not only is the finish very satisfying, but it is also quite a satisfying job in itself. Where the lawn has grown into the border, use a spade or half-moon edger to return the lawn's shape and to create a shallow 'moat' that the grass can't cross. Alternatively, you can install permanent edging, such as bricks or stone, that you can mow across.

To get the most thatch from your lawn, go over the area twice, first raking in one direction and then the other.

tip

Although it doesn't look that bad immediately, moss doesn't wear well and quickly turns brown at the first sniff of drought. Moss weedkillers are only a short-term solution, as they don't address the underlying problem of poor drainage and lack of food. The answer is spiking and brushing in fresh topsoil, as well as feeding your lawn a couple of times during summer to encourage strong growth.

SCARIFYING

If you fancy an autumn work out, one way of working up a sweat while you are improving the health of your lawn is to scarify it. Mow your lawn then take a spring-tine rake and scrape it vigorously over the surface, working your way across the lawn. This process pulls out the dead grass, known as 'thatch', which collects at the base of the grass blades.

As grass grows it piles up on top of itself leaving a layer of dead grass at the base. Grass clippings also fall down into it, stifling the air and light that reach the roots and preventing it from growing as thickly as it could. As well as removing all the dead matter and opening up the grass, scarifying stimulates young leafy growth at the expense of flowers, so helps to keep the grass juvenile.

It is amazing how much is produced and the scrapings are perfect for adding to the compost heap. For larger lawns, or for those gardeners less inclined to energetic activity, you can buy or hire an electric scarifier to save the blisters.

SPIKING

The path to the shed, the mouth of the football goal and the place where you stand to put the washing out are all areas where the soil can get compacted through use. If this happens the grass can stop growing so well, which leads to bare patches in the summer and mud baths in the winter. The solution is to relieve the compaction and aerate the soil by pushing a garden fork about 10cm (4in) deep into the soil every 10cm (4in) and gently rocking back and forth on the fork handle. The metal points open up the soil, allow the roots to breathe and encourage the grass to re-grow and fill gaps.

On heavy ground, such as clay soils, brush washed, sharp sand or fine horticultural grit into the holes to improve drainage and reduce future compaction.

Grass grows best on free-draining sandy soil. If your soil is heavy, after spiking brush a mixture of coir or leaf mould, loam and sharp sand (at the rate of 1:2:4) into the holes.

PESTS AND PROBLEMS

Most lawns are rarely troubled by serious fungal problems or infestations of grass-chewing grubs, but if it does happen it is best nipped in the bud to prevent spread and limit the damage so that it can be repaired.

ROOT-EATING GRUBS AND ANTS

If, around midsummer, you notice starlings or rooks are starting to peck at your soil and your lawn starts to develop dead and brown spots, then chances are you've got leather jackets (the larvae of daddy long legs) living in the soil under your lawn. If the same thing happens between late summer and spring then it's probably garden chafer grubs.

Regardless of the type of pest, the damage caused by their root chewing is the same and can be addressed by watering the lawn with a biological control called *Steirnernema carpocapsae*. These tiny, naturally occurring nematodes invade the bodies of the grubs and kill them. Water grass well before you apply the nematodes as it will help them to move around in the soil more effectively.

This organic solution is far better than using chemicals, which can also kill worms that are good for your soil and lawn. Another good organic method is to water the affected areas well and cover with plastic sheeting overnight. This brings the grubs to the surface so once you remove the cover in the morning they can be disposed of or left for the birds.

Colonies of ants also leave dead patches on the lawn, make it difficult to mow and can put you off your picnic. Again, a

TAKE YOUR OWN LAWN CUTTINGS

One of the most common lawn complaints is bare patches, usually caused by wear and tear or accidental damage by pets, kids or even accidental petrol spills while you are filling the mower. You can buy turf to replace these patches, but as there are hundreds of different blends of grass varieties it is unlikely you will be able to match your lawn. I solve this problem by making my own spare strips of grass from left-overs when I re-shape the lawn, and because they originally come from the lawn they always blend in seamlessly. Just collect up the strips and place them 5cm (2in) apart in a compost-filled seed-tray, then grow them on outside or in a cold frame. Keep the strips trimmed with shears and the grass will soon spread to cover the tray.

To replace the bare patch, cut out a square or rectangle around the area and, using a hand trowel, dig up the soil in the rectangle to whatever depth of

soil your new turf strip is. Gently rake the space over with your hand (a fork or rake for larger areas), and then lay the turf, cut to fit, over the patch. Firm it down using the flat of your hand so that there are no gaps and your new turf is no higher or lower than your existing lawn.

nematode comes to the rescue, *Steinernema feltiae,* which you water on, repeatedly if necessary, to drive the ants away. Don't use boiling water to combat the ant, although it is the best way to deal with nests in paved areas it will kill the grass.

FAIRY RINGS AND FUNGAL PROBLEMS

Fairy rings are strange concentric rings of dead and lush grass that sprout mushrooms in the autumn. They are caused by a fungus that spreads just below the soil, feeding some of the grass and robbing the dead patches of water. They aren't that common in gardens, but if you do get them you can only completely get rid of the problem by digging out the soil to a depth of 30cm (12in) and replacing the soil and grass. Alternatively, you can prevent the rings from spreading all over the lawn by removing the mushrooms when they appear in the autumn and by collecting the grass clippings separately and burning them.

Other fungal problems, such as Dollar spot, thatch fungus and Red Thread show up as dead spots, sometimes accompanied by mushrooms, often in the autumn. They're associated with a lack of air in the soil, so spiking and raking will help, and a lack of food, so apply a seaweed fertilizer in the autumn and increase the amount you feed your lawn in the summer.

PET TROUBLES

Male and female dog urine can kill your lawn, but the way female dogs squat and concentrate the ammonia in one place can cause brown dead patches. Watering to disperse the urine within an hour or two can help, but few people have time to be so vigilant. Some advocate creating a dog toilet of bark chips, but as the females like to vary where they go you will need at least 3m² (10ft²) of spare land, so it's not really an option in a small garden. Alternatively, you can buy a big bag of seed and keep raking out and over sowing the dead patches every few months. But in the end it might come down to compromise and which you love more – your dog or your lawn!

FROZEN FOOTPRINTS

Try not to walk on your lawn when it is frozen or frosted as the pressure of your foot can cause the frozen cells in the grass to melt rapidly, rupturing the walls and killing the grass. This can lead to a trail of dead 'footprints' across your lawn that is an invitation to mould. If you need to get rid of such a trail, rake out the dead grass and over sow it in spring.

FERTILIZER BURNS AND PETROL SPILLS

Any mysterious dead stripes or patches that appear after you have been tending the lawn can be down to accidental damage. Getting the application rate of your fertilizer wrong is a very common mistake if you are overgenerous or accidentally do the same place twice. If you realise you have made this mistake, immediately hose the area with water to dilute the feed and hope for the best. If you only spot the problem when the damage shows up, keep watering to try and alleviate the burning.

If you accidentally spill petrol on the grass while you are filling the mower, soak it up with an absorbent cloth. If the grass dies, however, the soil is poisoned and will need to be replaced before new seed is sown.

tip

Regularly move garden furniture and children's toys around the lawn to avoid killing off patches of grass. Once light and air gets back to the sward, yellowed grass will recover in a matter of days.

CHOOSING YOUR MOWER

If you aren't aiming for a perfect, bowling-green lawn then you should buy a rotary mower. They have blades that spin around, cutting the grass as it goes. You can lower the blades to create a reasonably neat finish, or raise them for tackling longer areas of grass and for first cuts. They are either electric- or petrol-powered, which is better for larger lawns. A more recent innovation is battery-powered mowers that have all the freedom of the petrol types (no cable), but are cleaner, quieter and rechargeable.

Choose the size of your mower to suit the size of your lawn. It might sound obvious, but bear in mind that although a wider mower will cut the lawn more quickly it will be heavier and bulkier to store, and not good at tight corners.

For a really fine finish and short grass, cylinder mowers with rotating blades, like a combine harvester, are the traditional and best choice. The action of the rotating cylinder snips the

HOW TO LEVEL DIPS AND DIVOTS

Bumps and hollows in a lawn can cause all sorts of problems, not least with ball games. They are difficult to mow neatly, and often cause your mower to scalp the grass, and are also trip hazards, even if they are useful scapegoats for poor performances at family games of croquet! It is possible to level them off though, here's how:

1 With a spade, slice an 'X' right across the centre of the sunken area. Then, just like lifting turf (see p25), gradually peel each triangle back to the level area. Don't worry if some of the turf rips, but try to remember how it fits back together.

2 Fork over the exposed soil and add some garden-centre bought loam or topsoil from a border. Rake it flat, firm it with your feet, add more soil to bring it up to the level of the surrounding soil (not to the top of the grass), and rake it flat.

3 Fold the peeled triangles of turf back down, patting them firmly level so their edges are in contact and there are no gaps for water to well up in.

grass like a pair of scissors. Over time, the blades on any mower will become blunt with wear and tear and they won't cut the grass so cleanly, so make sure you get the blades sharpened and balanced every year at a lawn-mower repair shop.

Some rotary mowers collect the cut grass and others mulch, shredding up the cut grass and letting it fall back into the lawn. Large lawns suit a mulching mower better, unless you want to spend a lot of time dumping and composting clippings, but the finish won't be as tidy. If you want a lawn with neat stripes, get a mower with a roller on the back.

For those with a large or sloping garden, consider getting a self-propelled or ride-on mower to make life easier. For grassy banks, where a ride-on would be dangerous, a hover mower that floats above its spinning, helicopter-like blades works well. Alternatively, invest in a strimmer; it won't produce a neat finish, but is brilliant for banks and for taming rough verges around the allotment.

HAVING FUN WITH YOUR LAWN

If you want to practise your mini-golf at home, it's simple to add a few golf holes using plant pots sunk into the lawn. I use 10cm (4in) terracotta pots as they are less flimsy and better looking than plastic ones, and it makes a satisfying plunk when you get a hole in one. Use a trowel to dig out a hole and set the pot so that the rim is at the same level as the soil surface. That way it won't catch the ball or your mower blades.

I know – any excuse to get out the drill and have a play. But I think the result is pretty good...

WILDLIFE

Birds and bees don't recognise fences as boundaries. As gardeners, tapping into that rare freedom can be both liberating and life-affirming, a touchstone that can connect us to a life outside the hustle and bustle of our own lives. The more you slow down and take notice, the more wildlife there is to see. Use it to inform your style of gardening, whether it means planting early spring flowers to feed bumble bees or leaving the ladybird larvae to take care of the aphids.

Encouraging wildlife into your garden is not entirely altruistic, however, and making this connection will also inform how you deal with the threats it brings to your plants. Observation teaches you the difference between a root-munching millipede and a harmless centipede – as will a well-illustrated wildlife and insect guide – while talking to seasoned gardeners at your local allotments or plant nursery will offer you myriad solutions. My answer is to embrace new natural technology, such as biological controls and plant tonics that boost plants' immune systems. Physical barriers, such as horticultural fleece, are also useful for keeping crops such as carrots healthy and pest-free, as is the age-old art of distraction; using companion plants that release scents and oils to deter or lure pests elsewhere. Using a combination of all these methods in a 'carrot' rather than a 'stick' way works best in any garden, but especially where you want to keep it natural.

MAINTAINING A NATURAL GARDEN

■ Choose the right plants. When it comes to choosing plants there is often a choice between 'natural' varieties – those closely related to wild species that are robust and hardy and have good disease resistance – and those selected for larger, brighter or more numerous flowers. Time was when all plants were bred to have increasingly unusual colours, often at the expense of other qualities. For example, in the 1970s and 1980s the big push among rose breeders was the development of the 'blue rose'. They got pretty close with *R*. Blue Moon, with petals the colour of a sucked blue Smartie, but in exchange for the washed-out blue petals, the growth was spindly and the leaves were disease prone. These days, breeders are still after interesting colours, but there is greater emphasis on disease resistance. You can pick out the best varieties by looking for the Royal Horticultural Society (RHS) Award of Garden Merit stickers on their labels. This award shows that the plant has been trialled in an RHS garden and performed above and beyond the call of duty.

■ Choose plants that grow well in the various microclimates in your garden. Avoid, for example, planting a rose that is prone to blackspot in a crowded airless border, or a sun-seeking rockrose in a shady place. Powdery mildew is prevalent on hot, dry sites so avoid susceptible species, such as *Clematis texensis*. Some plants grow better in certain areas, for example, Cox's Orange Pippin apples are prone to scab when they are grown in damp northern and western climates, but when grown in the east they do just fine. There are also diseases that attack in certain seasons, such as potato blight, which is prevalent in wet summers and can be avoided altogether by growing early 'new potato' crops.

■ Be aware of the seasons, as each one will pose its own problems – vine weevils attack in spring and autumn, and so does the biological control that kills the hatching grubs.

■ Patrol your crops regularly so you can spot potential problems early.

■ Break the cycle of pests by rotating crops so they don't grow in the same place year after year. If pests do build up, such as whitefly on brassicas, leave the patch empty for a month.

■ Keep the garden clean and tidy – if you pick up leaves and mummified fruits, you will prevent fungal diseases or re-infection if you have already had a problem.

ATTRACT WILDLIFE INTO YOUR GARDEN

The robins and blackbirds that accompany my digging, the hedgehogs that surprise me with their grunts and snuffles when I take out the rubbish, the hoverflies that dance above the fennel, all add an extra layer to my garden that is beyond my making and it is one for which I feel ultimately responsible. Our busy lives often mean we are too absorbed in our own world to notice what is going on around us, but just one day spent quietly enjoying and watching your garden will have you putting up bird feeders in no time.

BEES

When it comes to attracting bees it is not just what you grow, but how you grow it that matters. Groups of flowers are more attractive to bees as, like a one-stop-shop, the bees don't have to travel far to gather pollen and nectar. Choose plants with abundant flowers, such as cranesbill, echium and agastache, so the bees don't have to travel very far, and plants that bloom over a long period, such as *Verbena bonariensis*, catmint, perennial wallflowers and sedum.

There are 24 species of bumblebee in the UK, half a dozen of which are common in British gardens, but all of them are under threat due to intensive farming practices and a lack of wildflowers to provide food for them. As marshes, hedgerows and wildflowers disappear, so bees become more prone to extinction. (According to the Bumblebee Conservation Trust, two species have died out in the last 70 years.) Gardens have therefore become more important as providers of food, so at least there are things we can do to help.

■ Make sure you grow plenty of bee food – pollen and nectar. Pollen provides protein, so plant protein-rich species, such as members of the nettle family (deadnettles) and *Boraginacae* like echium and viper's bugloss.

■ Make room for some wildflowers, such as bluebells and foxgloves, which have more to offer bees than exotic species

that often have little nectar or pollen or may have complicated flowers that are inaccessible to our native bees.

■ Bees are out and about in the garden from March to September, so having flowers right through those months will ensure a rich harvest for them. I always know spring has sprung when I spot my first bumblebee, but that can be as early as February when not much is around so I have plenty of blossom from flowering currants, hellebores, pulmonaria and daffodils for them to feed on.

BIRDS

Birds aren't just beautiful to look at, robins, tits and finches eat aphids and caterpillars so they should all be encouraged. To encourage birds to visit after plants have finished flowering, rather than put the flowering stems on the compost heap, keep the seed-heads for the birds. Seed-packed sunflower heads make great homemade bird feeders, either hung from fences or put on the bird table, and fluffy, thistle-like globe artichokes are also a favourite nest-building material for finches. If it is possible, plant hedges over fences, particularly dense thorny types like thorny pyracantha, as they will not only act as a barrier to the wind, but also provide a safe place for birds to nest. Birds are

LEFT: Nectar-rich borage is loved by bees.

RIGHT: And for birds, home-made feeder tables and Nature's version, sunflower heads.

more likely to use a feeder or table if it is put an open spot where they can see cats coming. If there are trees nearby it gives birds a place to pause before swooping down to feed.

INSECTS

Leave hollow-stemmed plants standing in the borders through winter to provide a place for aphid-eating hoverflies, ladybirds and lacewings to overwinter. You can also buy custom-made insect boxes that are essentially like bird boxes, but instead of being empty the inside is filled with small tubes for the insects to hole up inside. I've made a whole neighbourhood at Greenacre using chopped down old bamboo canes, although a few holes drilled into a log work just as well. Always change the canes or log every summer to stop mites that prey on the insect larvae building up.

BUTTERFLIES

Butterflies like blooms made up of numerous small flowers. Buddleia is the best example, but they also like sedum, teasel, hebe, lavender, Michaelmas daisies, catmint and honesty. These flowers will feed the butterflies that fly over your fence, but to boost their numbers you also need to provide food for the caterpillars. A small wild area in the corner of your garden or allotment is good for this, as the stinging nettles that will grow there are a perfect food source for small tortoiseshell, peacock, comma and red admiral caterpillars. They become butterflies before midsummer when you can chop back the nettles to prevent them seeding. The caterpillars of Painted Ladies love creeping thistles, the small copper butterfly loves docks, and holly and ivy are where the holly blue butterfly lays its eggs.

HEDGEHOGS

Hedgehogs love compost heaps, wood stores and leaf bins. If one decides to make your garden its home you are lucky, as it will soon set about devouring your slugs. If you want to supplement its diet, feed it with cat food – not milk and bread as this upsets their stomach. Hedgehogs are woodland creatures that hibernate amongst leaves and twigs, and sadly often mistake autumn bonfire stacks as a good place to sleep away the winter.

Give them a chance to escape by collecting material for burning in one place, then transferring it to another before setting your fire. They are nocturnal creatures, so if you see one during the day it will probably not be very well or might be a juvenile that has been separated from its mother. Contact your local hedgehog sanctuary or the British Hedgehog Preservation Society for help and advice.

FROGS, TOADS AND POND LIFE

Even a tiny pond does wonders for connecting your garden to the wider world. I once made a pond in a barrel and the moment it was finished a dragonfly – an insect that neither my neighbours nor I had ever seen in our central city gardens – landed on the water lilies!

The power of water to attract wildlife is immense. Just an old washing-up bowl sunk into the soil up to the rim can make a hang out for frogs – frogs will spawn in a puddle so they don't need much water. I make these tiny ponds near the compost heap, where slugs and snails also congregate, to provide a watery oasis for frogs and toads to rest between eating molluscs. If they are sunk in a shady spot and topped up with rain they won't go stagnant and grasses will soon dip their roots in to keep the water clean.

tip

Don't handle frogs or toads unless they are in harm's way, as it is stressful for them and they are easily dropped. If you need to handle them always wear gloves, as some people are allergic to their skin.

The common frog – sadly not so common any more.

Raised beds are also good places for sinking small, ready-made ponds. Being raised, it brings the water to a height where it is more easily enjoyed and it is easier to prevent small children from falling in, though of course you should still be vigilant. They are easier to install than ponds with flexible liners, as you simply dig a hole and pop it in, making sure the rim is level. The plastic edge of a flexible liner is more difficult to disguise, but I use the rust-covered links of old ship chains and pieces of driftwood to create a seaside effect, and at the same time offer a slipway in and out of the water for frogs and toads.

Location is also important. Ideally a natural pond needs part-day shade and dappled light, as too much sunlight allows algae to bloom. If you are using a liner, make the pond as large as you can. The earthwork may look immense, but when the liner is hidden and the pond is filled with water the size always seems to shrink and can disappoint. Stack the topsoil separately from the inert subsoil so you can re-use the topsoil in your borders.

Plant marginal plants, such as corkscrew rush (dragonflies bask on these), water-forget-me-not and spring-flowering marsh marigold, at the water's edge. Marginal plants are good for the smallest of ponds and even containers, as they soak up excess nitrogen with their roots and help to prevent algae blooming. Plant deep-water perennials, such as dwarf pygmaea water-lilies, in the centre of the pond. Use an oxygenator, such as parrot's feather (*Myriophyllum aquaticum*), that floats just below the water surface and releases oxygen into the water. Make the centre of your pond at least 60cm (2ft) deep to ensure that the deepest part stays frost-free no matter how cold the weather gets. Make a shelf at the bottom of the pond to create different habitats, and provide a shallow edge so that wildlife can access the water and get out easily.

Don't add ornamental goldfish as they eat frog, dragonfly, newt and insect eggs, instead make a separate pond for fish. To introduce micro-organisms that will help keep your pond healthy, seed your pond with a few bottles of water collected from an established, healthy wildlife pond – contact your local Wildlife Trust for advice on their locations if you don't have one locally. In no time at all your pond will be alive with water boatmen, water beetles and pond skaters, and come spring it will attract frogs to spawn.

tip

Frogs look very different to toads, they are smooth and leap about, whereas toads are larger, have rough, warty skin and move around by scrambling and walking.

COMPANION PLANTING

Of all the gardening hints, tips and rules, there's one that stands head and shoulders above the rest: 'work with nature and you won't go far wrong'. Companion planting is a way of doing just that – partnering up crops with friendly neighbours in order to discourage pests and encourage growth. It's a technique that has been around for generations, cleverly harnessing the tricks that plants employ to survive and compete in the wild. All it takes is a bit of matchmaking when you sow or plant.

Companion planting works by creating diversity and breaking up monocultures (large areas that are dedicated to one plant), which reduces the chances of crop-ruining infestations. They also provide one or more of the following:

African marigolds make a clear, colourful edging for veg plots, and they attract hoverflies that patrol your crops for aphids.

■ **Shelter, shade and support.** Tall annual plants, such as sunflowers, make good bedfellows in a kitchen garden because their tall leafy stems create beneficial shade for summer salad crops. They also make good windbreaks and climbing frames for runner beans and gourds.

■ **Space savings.** Some vegetables make such comfortable companions that they can share the same soil, thus increasing the variety of crops that can be grown on one patch, even in small areas. Planting strongly scented plants, such as chives, onions and marigolds, can also help to mask vulnerable crops from pests. Good examples are carrots combined with onions; the onions mask the scent of the carrots, making it harder for carrot fly to find them. Also, lettuce will produce a fast harvest planted on bare ridges of soil before potatoes leaf over the space.

■ **Predator homes.** Plants that die down for the winter, such as fennel, sunflowers, and Jerusalem and globe artichokes, often leave dead, hollow stems, which make useful hibernating homes for aphid-eating ladybirds and lacewings. In the spring they will wake up and patrol your plants, just as aphid numbers start to build up. Lacewings, in particular, lay eggs that give rise to voracious, insect-eating young – as well as killing caterpillars, lacewing larvae can gobble up to 100 aphids an hour! Ladybirds also like hibernating in semi-evergreen, felt-like foliage, such as stachys and leyland hedges. Ladybirds will hole up under windowsills and in sheds, too.

■ **Predator lures.** Trap plants work by enticing pests away from your precious crops and concentrating them in one place, which makes them easier to kill. Marigolds, for example, will draw slugs from your lettuce because the slugs find them even tastier than the lettuce, while nasturtiums will tempt black aphids from your broad beans.

■ **Fast food.** Members of the legume family, such as beans, clover and peas, trap nitrogen from the air, transport it to their roots and turn it into a form that's accessible to other plants. This makes them ideal partners for plants such as sweet corn and cabbage that require large amounts of nitrogen to grow well. Grow legumes in advance, leave their roots in the soil and plant the main crop around their spent stems.

■ **Natural chemicals.** All plants release chemicals from their roots that help support beneficial fungi in the soil. African marigolds also produce a nematode repellent (there are bad nematodes as well as good ones!) called thiopene that will drive the plant-eating, microscopic worms from your beds. Many American organic farmers use grain rye clippings to mulch around established tomatoes and cabbages, as it suppresses weeds by releasing a chemical that stops seeds from sprouting. While artemisias, such as Southern wormwood, have scented foliage that is laced with natural insecticide compounds that deter insects and slugs and help mask the scent of crops.

USE DISEASE-RESISTANT PLANTS

Disease resistance is the Holy Grail when it comes to selecting the vegetables and plants for your garden. This tactic will help you to avoid inherent problems later on.

Seed catalogues are the best places to research and find disease-resistant vegetables, for example, varieties of carrot that have been bred and selected for their resistance to carrot root fly. For flower, shrubs and trees look out for the RHS Award of Garden Merit that relate to their garden worthiness, you'll find this marked on the labels of plants in nurseries and garden centres. My trick for finding suitable fruit varieties is to think local and seek advice from specialist nurseries; they will know what traditionally grows well in different postcodes.

NATURAL SPRAYS AND TONICS

There are a whole range of relatively new organic products, known as natural plant improvers, tonics or invigorators, that are a cross between a fertilizer and a pesticide. The industry is still in its infancy, but there are already professional products available that use garlic and citrus as foliar fruit tree sprays and rabbit repellents. To date, few products are readily available to amateurs, but you can get hold of the ones I mention here via the Internet.

These tonics and invigorators are either applied to the soil to boost the microbiology and make nutrients more quickly available to the roots, or as liquids that are sprayed as a preventative onto plant foliage throughout the growing season, in much the same way that chemicals were used when we didn't know better, only this time without harming the environment. Both application methods have a dual action; boosting growth and warding off pests and diseases organically.

Sometimes you don't need any kind of product to stop pests. All you need to do is to rub them off by hand, or with a blast from the hose-pipe. It's all part of the new style of preventative organic gardening, which looks set to become common practice.

MYCORRHIZAL GRANULES

Although you may not have heard of them, mycorrhizal granules (a form of 'friendly fungus') have been around for some time and are used by many of the top horticultural organizations, including the RHS. Mycorrhizae develop naturally in the soil when plants grow from seed, but can be slow to start when used with pot-grown and bare-root plants. Mycorrhizal granules (available via mail order and from garden centres), hasten a plant's growth and boosts its establishment, and are applied directly to the roots at planting time. The plant and the mycorrhizae have a symbiotic relationship, each benefitting the other creates a secondary, larger root system that helps to gather more nutrients and water.

This friendly fungus has been shown to help with 'soil sickness', a condition where the earth in borders won't support growth. This often happens where one particular plant has been grown in a single spot for a long time, such as apple trees in orchards. It is also useful for hungry plants, such as roses, that are growing in poor sandy or chalky soils. I use it for planting new hedges, large shrubs or trees and roses to give these long-term, expensive plants a good start.

SOFT SOAP INVIGORATORS

The traditional soft soap spray (or surfactant) is a dilute detergent; a potassium-based fatty acid that damages the skins of sap-sucking insects, such as aphids and whitefly. It is less toxic than a chemical insecticide and also less effective, which means it is best used to nip infestations in the bud, but if it is used in large amounts it can damage the leaf cuticles of the plant.

A new generation of surfactants, based on plant foods, are now coming to the fore and being widely used by professionals; they are also available by mail order for amateurs. Like a cross between a nitrogen fertilizer and a natural pesticide/fungicide, they act on the outer skin of insects, such as whitefly, either making it sticky (gluing pests to one spot) or allowing water into the insects so that they drown. It also picks up fungal spores and washes them off before they have a chance to enter the leaves.

These plant invigorators are supplied as a concentrated liquid that is diluted and sprayed weekly onto the foliage of vulnerable plants. They work well against aphids, scale, bay sucker, spider mite, mealy bug, greenfly, and whitefly and can also be used to prevent powdery mildew on roses. It is also harmless to bees.

NEEM

Another organic invigorator is neem, a product that is made from the seeds of the neem tree (*Azardirachta indica*), which is the country cousin of the mahogany tree and is known as the

LEFT: Freshly boiled water kills ants in paving and patios.

RIGHT: seaweed tonic can be applied to foliage with a spray or a rose fitted to a watering can.

'Divine Tree' in India because of its cure-all properties. The oil can be bought via the Internet and sprayed directly onto the plant or applied as mulch. It contains a chemical called azadirachtin that not only contains a spectrum of plant nutrients, but also acts as a natural insect repellent by entering into the plant's sap and deterring sap-sucking insects.

I have used it as mulch on a viburnum which always gets blackfly and the results so far have been good. If it is applied every spring it should keep the pests away. Be aware that the mulch has a strong incense smell and should never be eaten, so pets and children need to be kept away from it. Pregnant women should also take care due to the essential oils it contains. It is safe to use on vegetables though.

SEAWEED TONIC

Seaweed tonic is a personal favourite of mine; it is high in potassium and packed with trace elements and micro-minerals that aren't available in an ordinary inorganic, chemical fertilizer and that boost the lustre of a plant. I spray it once a fortnight on my roses, right through the growing season, to boost their growth. It thickens the cuticles or glossy outer skin of the leaves, reducing their vulnerability to blackspot. I also use it as a feed for all my pot plants and vegetables. You can buy it in concentrated form from the garden centre or online; dilute it in a watering can and use as you would a tomato fertilizer.

WATER

Ordinary water can sometimes be extremely effective in the battle against pests. Hosing down plants and their environment can help to alter a pest's preferred habitat, for example, damping down the floor and plants in a greenhouse helps to get rid of red spider mites that thrive in a dry environment.

A sharp jet of water can also blast aphids off foliage, killing them in the process. I've even known gardeners clear infestations in trees, particularly woolly aphids, using a pressure washer. But don't get to close or you might take off the bark! Boiling water is the tried-and-tested trick for getting rid of ants nests on patios and in paving. Alternatively, leave the hosepipe gently trickling into their nest and they'll soon clear off.

BY HAND

Many pests are visible to the naked eye and can be literally nipped on the bud with your finger and thumb, before their numbers escalate out of control. This is a good trick for aphids that congregate around flower buds. Leaf miners are another pest that can be dealt with by hand. They tunnel through the leaves of fuchsias, hellebores and walnut trees, to name a few, leaving a marbled effect on the surface. The best way to combat them is to remove the affected foliage, pest, disease and all. With lily beetle, wipe off the tell-tale bird-poo-like larvae that lurk under the leaves, and be quick to squash any of the shiny red beetles that might fall from the plant and play dead on the soil.

Often fungal diseases are caused by damp or stagnant air, so a bit of judicious pinching-out can remove the source of infection and increase air circulation through the plant. Some plants, such as aquilegia, sweet Williams, valerian, catmint and oriental poppies, can succumb to mildew midseason, so these are best chopped back to the crown after they have flowered to rejuvenate them. This will produce a fresh, mildew-free set of leaves and sometimes even a second set of flowers.

BIOLOGICAL CONTROL VERSUS CHEMICALS

Not all wildlife is welcome and as a gardener you have to manage the creatures that would seek to devour everything you want to grow, but this needn't mean you have to garden in against nature.

Biological controls are a relatively new approach to dealing with pests, and these work by increasing the numbers of natural predators in order to reduce the number of pests. It is a holistic approach to the old chemical method that sought to indiscriminately eliminate everything. Biological control only works if pests and predators live in balance with one another. This means there will always be a few pests but damage will usually be minimal. Ultimately, biological controls are far better than using chemicals, as poison will never kill all the 'nasties' and they can even build up resistance, which can result in entire populations of pests that are immune to the chemicals designed to kill them. Worse still, because the natural predators are eating poisoned pests – a hedgehog eating a slug killed by methiocarb, for example – the natural predators are also likely to be affected by the chemicals, leaving surviving or resistant pests completely unchecked.

Some biological controls only work if chemical pesticides aren't and haven't recently been used in the greenhouse, as they can be sensitive to some chemical residues. They are sold via mail order, either from the Internet, gardening catalogues or as empty-box schemes from garden centres (where you buy the box and the bio-control is sent to you in the post).

But you can't talk about dealing with pests in a garden without mentioning chemicals. Though I spent years using them as a professional gardener, I don't use them anymore. Whether we like it or not, the writing is on the wall for this type of pest control, not least because of EU legislation curbing their use by amateur gardeners. The good news is that lots of new eco options are being introduced all the time. In the meantime, many gardeners still use chemicals because although prevention is always better than cure, it is not always possible.

If you are cornered and you feel you have no option but to use chemicals, use them carefully by spraying in the evenings after the bees have returned to their hives and nests and avoid using weedkiller sprays on breezy days to prevent drift. Never use chemicals near water as they are super-toxic to aquatic life. It sounds obvious, but always read the label and follow instructions as the doses are critical and misuse can scorch foliage and damage the environment. Also, only use 'pet-safe' options and keep children well away from where chemicals are used and stored.

NEMATODES

Nematodes are microscopic, worm-like predators that occur naturally in the soil. They are bought in packs, mixed in a clay dust, and should be kept in the fridge. When you are ready to use them, mix the contents of the pack in a watering can of water and pour it onto the soil or plant foliage. The tiny killers

tip

All biological controls are safe to use around children and pets, work well in wet weather and are safe to use on your edible crops.

NATURAL BARRIERS

Prevention is better than cure, so physically separating your crops from the pests or the vagaries of the weather is the one of the greenest ways to ensure perfect plants. You don't have to keep your plants covered all the time, but if you cover them strategically, for example overnight to keep off frosts or when particular pests are about, it will make a difference to how your garden grows.

■ **Horticultural fleece.** This opaque, light-filtering material is sold off the roll at garden centres, or in packs from mail-order companies. It has two main uses: keeping the frost and cold off tender plants early and late in the year (in winter it can also be used to wrap up palms and banana plants) and physically stopping sap-sucking insects such as caterpillars and flea beetle from attacking vegetables. Allotment keepers should always have a supply of fleece to hand, and a few handy bricks or stones to weigh it down. Pin it over carrot seedlings to keep off carrot fly, ward off flea beetle from cabbage plants in spring and later to prevent the cabbage white butterfly from laying their eggs on the leaves.

■ **Crop protection mesh.** Mesh works similarly to fleece, but it is more expensive as it is more robust and durable, and therefore better on windy sites. It is best used in conjunction with a rigid structure, such as hoops.

■ **Gritty mulches.** Coffee grounds, cocoa shells, crushed shell, gravel, or any other sharp or gritty substrate can be used as effective mulches for deterring slugs and snails. Scatter it around the crown of the plant, 1–2cm (½–¾in) thick so it completely girdles the plant. Make sure the leaves do not create a 'bridge' over the mulch, allowing a safe-crossing for slugs and snails.

■ **Grease bands.** Bought either as a 'glue' for smearing around the trunk or as packs of ready-made bands covered in a sticky, non-drying, natural grease, these bands prevent the wingless, female winter moth from climbing up into the branches and laying her eggs, which hatch into maggots and devour the fruit. Simply tie the band to the trunks and stakes of fruit trees in the autumn. Grease bands placed around the legs of greenhouse staging is also a good way of stopping vine weevils from climbing up and into pots.

■ **Plastic collars.** Make your own environmentally friendly barrier by cutting rings out of plastic drink bottles. Use them to encircle young seedlings to prevent slug and snail attack, as they won't like climbing over the sharp edge of the ring.

LEFT: Nematodes come in sachets mixed with clay which are added to water and poured onto soil or sprayed onto plants.

RIGHT: Spraying nematodes onto cabbages in the fight against cabbage white caterpillars.

will then seek out the pests and either kill them directly or destroy them by releasing bacteria that will stop the pests from feeding. Once the number of pests is reduced the number of the nematodes will also go down, thus creating a natural balance. The following pests can be controlled using nematodes:

SLUGS

Soil-dwelling slugs that organic pellets cannot reach often gnaw plants such as delphiniums, primulas and lupins. I use nematodes as an instant layer of protection in new areas of the garden, where the slug population is naturally very high. But remember it won't kill snails. Apply the nematodes in the spring, once the grass has started to grow and temperatures are above 5°C (41°F). This is when plants are small and very susceptible to slug damage. See p.30 for more tips on controlling slugs and snails.

ANTS

Nematodes are useful where you can't pour boiling water over the nest and where they are in inaccessible places, such as under the patio. They will act as a deterrent rather than killing them, but if you apply where and when they are a problem it will help to keep colonies at bay.

VINE WEEVILS

This can be a real problem following a mild winter. Tell-tale signs that you have an infestation of the root-chewing larvae are when you see the adult beetles on the plant, or even in the house. The beetles are about 1cm (½in) long, with dusty brown spotted backs and a distinctive long 'nose'. The brown-headed, white larvae live in the soil and are also about 1cm (½in) long. If you notice your plants wilting, even when the soil or compost is wet, then the grubs may be at work destroying the roots. Pot plants are particular targets, particularly those grown in open, peaty composts, so adding loam to your pot composts can be a good preventative. Biological control with nematodes will work outside in temperatures above 5°C (41°F), and all year round in the greenhouse. The best time to apply it is April and September, to coincide with the natural egg-laying and hatching period of the beetle.

CATERPILLARS

Biological control of caterpillars is particularly useful on windy or ornamental sites where fleece can blow away or look messy. It also comes into its own on allotments, where the number of caterpillars can reach epidemic proportions. It is good for brassicas and also works well on codling moths, the grubs of which live in apples and pears and gooseberry sawfly larvae. Spray the foliage with nematodes when you first see caterpillars attacking the leaves.

CHAFER GRUBS AND LEATHERJACKETS

In late summer these root-chewing, pale, leathery-larvae can cause whole areas of lawn to first turn brown then die off, and are a recurring problem in some gardens. Chafer grubs are 'C'-shaped with brown heads and leatherjackets are about 2.5cm (1in) long with a dirty, grey-brown body and a dark head. Nematodes can be applied to deal with both of these pests in early autumn before the soil temperature drops below 10°C (50°F). Alternatively, where lawn has been lifted for new borders, the best solution is to keep digging the soil to expose the grubs that then make a tasty snack for the birds.

BAY SUCKER

This pest resembles small lentils. They live clustered on stems and the undersides of leaves and are difficult to kill because of the hard shell that they live under. Bay suckers lay huge amounts of eggs that hatch into 'crawlers' and move around the plant to find a suitable spot to set up home, before growing a hard shell. Nematodes are your best method of attack. Spray them onto the infected foliage and keep the crown covered with a plastic bag for 12 hours to keep the foliage wet so the nematodes can swim to find their prey. Three doses are usually needed to clear up a particularly nasty infestation.

FUNGAL DISEASES

Fungal diseases, such as mildew, are weather and microclimate-related, but you can help prevent many of them by simply not over planting or allowing plants to become too crowded, particularly fruit and vegetables. Fruit trees and bushes should be pruned (see p.168) to allow air to circulate through the branches. With roses, another plant that is particularly susceptible to fungal disease, choose disease-resistant varieties and give them the five-star planting treatment with plenty of soil improver and fungal mycorrhizae (see p.222). Also choose disease-resistant climbers and prune them to allow plenty of air circulation, particularly where they are planted against hot walls and fences. Train their stems onto wires, held proud of the wall by vine-eyes. And if you must grow old favourites, accept that you will need to use a fungicide preventatively throughout the season.

You will know you have an outbreak of fungal disease when the leaves of your plants look off-colour and are covered with spots and blotches. It is tempting to try to boost the plant's immunity with a feed, but if you had the flu would you fancy a three-course dinner? Sick plants are best left unfed, as even moderate levels of nitrogen will encourage new soft growth that will be even more vulnerable to fungal attack. It is better to water carefully, keeping the leaves dry to prevent spread, and mulch with garden compost to slowly improve growing conditions.

Simple ways to stop re-infection are to collect any mummified fruit from the branches and around fruit trees and to clear infected leaves, both on the plant and particularly when they fall, to prevent them from becoming a source of re-infection. You can put mildewed leaves on the compost heap, even a cold one, provided it is covered, but woody stems are always best burnt because they won't readily rot down.

WHITEFLY

Whiteflies are relatives of aphids. They are conspicuous by the white casings that are dropped by the immature nymphs as they grow, and by the way they fly up in plumes when infested plants are disturbed. Like all aphids they suck sap and deposit a sugary substance that turns to black mould. Whitefly is not easy to eradicate, but a tiny parasitic wasp called *Encarsia formosa* can be an effective biological solution. It comes as pupae in a sachet that you hook onto the stems of plants in the greenhouse – it won't work outside because they just fly away. Although *Encarsia* is a wasp, it doesn't sting and only attacks whitefly eggs. Use it when the temperature is above 10°C (50°F), and as soon as the whitefly appear. Whitefly aren't such a problem outside, but to control their numbers use a soft soap invigorator (see p.223) or spray plants such as cabbage with a hose to disrupt and drown the insects.

Whitefly on the underside of cabbage leaves.

LIVING IN YOUR GARDEN

PART THREE

GARDEN PROJECTS

Gardens are one of the best places for open-ended, non-prescriptive play… and that's just for the adults! Where else can you muck around, break the rules and experiment? Your garden needn't be just a museum of plants; instead the whole space can be a workshop for your ideas. The place to make useful stuff, such as structures to hide bins, presses to squeeze juice from your windfalls, or tunnels where the children can play among the supports for your French beans and runners. Lovely though plants are to look at, they also offer great potential for fun – tree swings and climbing nets are a great way to lure your children away from the TV and computer games, and you can also make your garden a real haven for the grown ups, too. I expect my garden to recapture the outdoor freedom I experienced as a child, the thrill of having a space to call your own, and more importantly to make your own. After all, the more time you spend in your garden the better you will be at understanding it, which will ultimately turn you into a better gardener. The joy is all in the doing.

CHILD'S PLAY

Children can find opportunities for play in the most innocuous things. My favourite types of garden toys are those that integrate with the garden, such as climbing nets and wooden swings slung from trees, rather than the shop-bought, plastic horrors that are just plonked on the lawn. Not only do they look better, but there's the magic of playing in and amongst the plants under clear blue skies that creates memories that last a lifetime.

COOL CLIMBING NETS
If your woodwork skills won't stretch to making a bespoke tree house, a cargo-net draped between the boughs of a tree is the next best thing. Like giant webs made from sturdy woven nylon, cargo-nets are ideal for scrambling up or just lolling about amongst the branches.

The best place to buy them is in an army surplus store where they sell all manner of useful outdoor kit and caboodle that the military no longer needs. As you would expect from a net designed to wrap and lug army equipment around, it will easily bear the weight of several adults and children.

I bought one as a present for my youngest son and strung it up in an old apple tree where it has occupied the kids and their friends for hours. Unlike so many other brightly coloured garden toys, it camouflages well with its surroundings. And in fruit trees like mine it's not just good for play, it makes picking the apples much easier and safer than clambering around in the branches.

MAKE A PULLEY CABLECAR

Pulleys have a Chitty Chitty Bang Bang charm to them and are brilliant for delivering toys and sweets to treetop hideouts. They can also be useful for shade-sails and privacy screens, taking the strain out of lifting a heavy compost bin lid and hoisting heavy hanging baskets above head height.

For a cable-car style you'll need two pulleys, one on either side of the garden, connected by a loop of thick twine. Buy them from chandlers (better quality than DIY stores). Lash a bucket to the twine and your children can transport their valuables from place to place.

MAKE A TREE SWING

1 Apart from a sturdy tree branch to hang it on, all you need to make a timber swing is a piece of timber, roughly 5cm (2in) thick and 22cm (8½in) wide – conveniently the size of an off-cut of reclaimed scaffold board. Cut it to the length you want the seat – 60cm (2ft) is about right for one person. Drill four holes, one in each corner, 3cm (1¼in) from the edge using a 15mm drill bit. Then sand the wood down to remove any splinters.

2 I prefer a rustic look so I use 15mm polyhemp rope – it looks similar to old sailor's rope, but has all the strength of a manmade fibre. You need two equal lengths of rope, with enough to go from the branch to the ground, plus another 1.5m (5ft) for knots. The best knot to use to attach to the top of the rope to the tree is called a 'Fisherman's Bend'. Take the end of the rope loosely around the branch twice, push the end back through both loops and then tie the loose end to the hanging rope as shown (1).

3 To attach the seat, tie a figure-of-eight knot in your ropes and take the end down through and back up the holes on each side of the seat. Secure the rope by pushing the end up and around the original figure-of-eight knot (2). Repeat on the other side, adjust the heights of the knots to get the seat level and pull tight (3).

A HAVEN FOR GROWN-UPS

The fun to be had from a garden isn't just in the gardening. I use mine as a workshop for tinkering and making stuff – not all of it welcome I might add – but at least it's not cluttering up the living room! This is how you make use of all those bits and pieces that you can't help collecting. Some of the simplest things to make are garden seats, shelves and bird tables, while some, like my apple press, may take a bit more fiddling with, but at least the rewards are delicious.

MAKE A DRIFTWOOD AND RECLAIMED TIMBER BENCH

I made this bench from an old pallet and pieces of sea-washed driftwood I found washed up after a storm on my local beach, but if you can't get to the coast you could equally use sun-bleached timber sourced from a woodland trust or local tree surgeon. The beauty of a bench you make yourself is that no two will ever be the same, and it also doubles up as a piece of homemade garden.

Chop down the pallet to make the seat – mine is a 'D' shape – then cut some sturdy legs, either from off-cuts or use 10cm (4in) fence posts. The finished height of the seat should be about 40cm (16in) off the ground. Fix the legs to the base of the seat using L-shaped, metal brackets (available from any builders' merchant). Use decking screws to fix the driftwood to the pallet frame and then wire them tightly to the timber for strength. You can disguise the wire with old rope and hide the screws by smearing putty over the top of them. For an artistic finish you can also clad the pallet legs with more pieces of driftwood.

MAKE A HOMEMADE JUICE PRESS

The garden, rather than the kitchen, is the best place to tackle the messy job of pressing fruit to make juice. I do it every autumn to make the most of the mountain of windfalls from my old apple tree and over the years I have perfected the technique. First I freeze and thaw the fruit to make the apples soft and yielding. Then I use the pressing power of a car-jack, which is far cheaper than an expensive, purpose-made press, to collect buckets of apple juice.

To make a homemade press, first put together a frame (60cm (2ft) wide and 75cm (30in) tall) from 8cm (3in) thick posts, fixed together with wood glue and bolts; or proper timber joints if your woodworking skills are good enough. Once you have your frame bolt on legs, made from off-cuts of timber from the frame, for

stability and cut two chunky slabs of timber 10 x 30 x 30cm (4 x 12 x 12in) to fit between the frame uprights to create 'jaws' that will squeeze down on the fruit.

Thaw the frozen apples by dropping them into a bucket of water. When they are soft, wrap five at a time in a piece of muslin or an old tea towel – this will prevent the apples from escaping when they are being pressed. Place the wrapped apples between the two chunky timber 'jaws', put your car jack on top of the upper piece of chunky timber and brace the jack against the frame. Wind the jack and watch the juice flow!

I store juice for the winter by pouring it into washed plastic milk bottles and freezing it. It has become our family tradition to serve it up, first thing, on Christmas morning.

MAKE A FRONT-GARDEN BIN STORE

I'm a big fan of recycling, but even I struggle with the number of boxes, bins and bags required to separate up the rubbish. A timber bin store can bring order to chaos, while also looking good.

Every council has a different system and number of bins – my store holds two wheelie bins and two recycling boxes. It is built from reclaimed timber and has a green roof to integrate it with the garden. If you are buying new materials, choose treated, rough-sawn fence gravel boards and fence posts.

The wheelie bin store has a palisade gate, clad with timbers, that is high enough to hide the two bins. I didn't put a roof on it, as it would make it hard to open the lids of the wheelie bins. The adjacent box store has a roof, topped with green roof matting, and is made up of a framework of fence posts and has a shelf made from gravel boards to keep recycled papers dry. I put an angled top on the box store to help hide the bins and show off the green roof. The roof can be any angle you like, but to get the same angle on all your cuts, make a template out of a spare piece of wood first and use this to mark up your timber before sawing. For stability I screwed my bin store to the garage, but for free-standing structures you can use a quick-setting concrete mix to secure the base of the posts into the soil.

GREEN ROOFS

A green roof is a drought-tolerant mix of stonecrops (*Sedum*), a species that is adapted to living on mountains and is ideal for greening up hostile places like shed roofs, animal hutches and garden offices. The cheapest way is to grow your own is by propagating succulent plants bought from the alpine section of the garden centre in trays of 50:50 Perlite and multipurpose compost, grown outside in the sun. More expensive, but far easier, is to buy them by the metre or foot as ready-grown mats. Either way, the effect is immediate and, with minimal care

MAKE A HAZEL TUNNEL

A hazel tunnel is a fun and useful way to connect different parts of the garden or to instantly create height, as it is just the place for growing climbing beans, sweet peas or ornamental gourds. It takes just two hours to make and will last for two years or more before it starts to fall apart and has to be fixed or replaced.

Use 3m (9ft) hazel or sweet chestnut poles about 2.5–8cm (1–3in) thick from a local woodland trust. Make sure the wood is freshly cut, so it is bendy enough to make the arches. The tunnel can be as long as you like, but for stability it should ideally be at least 120cm (4ft) wide.

Using a crow bar, make two opposite rows of holes every 30–40cm (12–16in), and push a hazel pole into each hole. Gently bend the tops of the opposite poles together to meet and create an arch. Tie them together with twine. To make sure the arches are even, tie a straight pole between the front and back arch and adjust the middle arches so that they fit neatly beneath it. Secure the arches to the top pole with more twine.

Add more horizontals, as shown, to make square windows down the sides, and lash on a diagonal pole (pushed into the soil at one end) to give the tunnel rigidity. Finally, plant climbing beans and gourds at the base of the poles and train them up so they clad the sides and drape from the arches.

(the occasional water when it's dry and an annual feed with slow-release fertilizer), it will last for years.

For any green roof you need to create a tray with 50mm (¾in) raised timber sides to cover the roof and hold the plants in place. Protect the timber tray by tacking a plastic sheet, or old compost bag for small roofs, to the sides of the tray. Next, put a drainage layer, such as Perlite, sand or a mat supplied by a green roof specialist, followed by capillary matting that has been pre-soaked in a bucket of water. Tack the matting down and lay the green roof mat on top. All the layers, including the green roof, can be cut to size using a craft knife.

EAT, DRINK AND BE MERRY

Cooking and eating outdoors always feels special, even celebratory. I love everything about it, from preparing fuss-free and washing-up-free children's food like bangers and baps, to larger, more involved meals, made to feed large gatherings of friends and family.

It's these outdoor feasts that I've concentrated on in this chapter – food with a wow factor that's easy to prepare and won't mean you're chained to the barbecue while it cooks. Herbs and vegetables you've grown yourself always taste better than anything you buy, particularly when cooked out in the appetite-boosting fresh air. And the pleasure isn't just in the eating; it's also in the anticipation – in my house, gathering in the ingredients for Christmas dinner has become as much a festive tradition as going and getting the tree and hanging up the decorations. What's more, being outside in the fresh air on an adventure in squally weather is a brilliant antidote to what can so easily become a commercial and pre-packaged Christmas.

THE OUTDOOR KITCHEN

It always feels like a celebration when you eat outdoors, and with our uncertain summer weather you have to take your chances when you can. Flavours take on an extra dimension – they are more aromatic and fresh – plus there's an added satisfaction if it's homegrown food. Personally, I prefer to feed the kids outside because there's less clearing up to do!

CELEBRATE!

Plants ring the year's changes and there's one to celebrate every season. Sowing your own pumpkin in spring, for example, rather than buying it from the supermarket for Halloween sets up a delicious anticipation of the fun to come. It also gives your garden plants a value. Whether it's cutting a sprig of holly at Christmas or bunches of hydrangea flowers to decorate a birthday party, these acts become family rituals that embellish your home and enrich your life.

BUILD A HANGI

You don't necessarily need a barbecue to cook outdoors – if you think like a Maori, you can cook in the soil. My good friend Richard introduced me to the New Zealand 'hangi', which is a temporary underground oven.

Start this project on the morning you want to eat by digging a hole 90cm (3ft) wide and 60cm (2ft) deep. It is best to locate it away from your house, at the bottom of your garden, and make sure it is away from fences, overhanging foliage and buildings. Build and light a fire next to the hole, and as it burns pile up 15–20 large stones (not so heavy you struggle to lift them) or bricks into the fire so they heat up. Keep the fire blazing for an hour or two, by adding more wood or barbecue coals, while you prepare your food.

Hangis are ideal for cooking joints of meat as they slow-cook the cuts, which holds in all the moisture and flavour. To keep the meat off the soil, and to make moving it easier once cooked, you will need a wire basket – an old supermarket-style shopping basket will do, or you can fashion your own from chicken wire. Line the basket with an old, soaking-wet sheet (I used an old curtain); then add a layer of cabbage leaves on top of the sheet as a bed for the meat.

Place the meat on top of the cabbage leaves – here it is lamb, flavoured with garlic and rosemary from the garden and packed around with carrots, onions and leeks from the allotment. Cover the meat and vegetables with more cabbage leaves and swaddle the whole thing in the wet sheet.

Back at the fire, wearing gloves use a spade to move the hot stones into the base and up the sides of the hole. Cover them with a wet sheet and lower your foodbasket into the middle. Place another wet sheet over the basket and cover the whole thing with soil. Leave it to slow-cook for five to seven hours. This is great for parties because there is a huge element of anticipation when you finally bring the cooked food out of the ground and the fresh herbs add to the delicious smells.

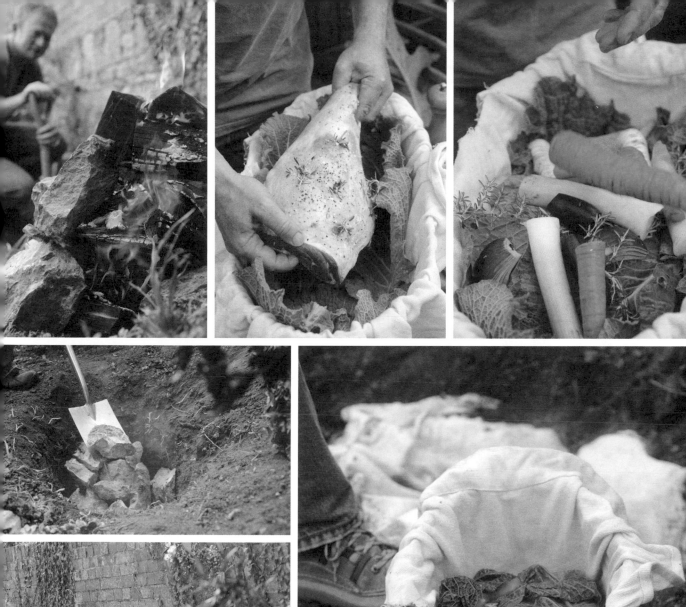

ROAST CHICKEN IN A BARBECUE

As much as I love to barbecue you can end up spending a lot of time standing over it with staggered food delivery and guests eating at different times. I prefer roasting a whole chicken on my barbecue; it gives you that great charcoal taste and smell without all the work.

You need a kettle-style barbecue, with a lid, and you need to make sure it is nice and hot before you put the chicken inside. Arrange the barbecue coals in a thick ring around the outside, leaving space in the centre for a bowl of water – I make the bowl myself from folded tinfoil. As the heat is around the chicken, and not under it, fat from the cooking chicken drops into the water rather than onto burning coals, which would create an unpleasant, acrid smoke. The chicken will be ready in the same time as it would if you were cooking it in the oven.

I flavour my bird with an 'American butt rub' – a Texan recipe given to me by an American friend. Put a large handful of finely chopped fresh oregano leaves, two finely sliced onions, a couple of garlic cloves, a teaspoon of smoked paprika and seasoning into a bowl. Mix the ingredients into a paste with some olive oil and rub it all over and under the skin on the breast of the chicken.

To add an authentic, sweet, smoky flavour I chop up freshly-cut twigs from my apple tree, wrap them in tinfoil, puncture the foil with a couple of holes in the top and place them on the coals to smoulder. If you use old dead wood, soak it in water first or it will just burn up.

tip

To get charred oil off your barbecue grill, rub half an onion over the metal when it is hot. The acidic juice of the onion will quickly get the grill squeaky clean.

Pumpkin 'Rouge Vif d'Etampes' carved Swiss-cheese style for Halloween.

HALLOWEEN

For a guide to growing your own pumpkins see p.137. The best varieties for Halloween lanterns are the big'uns – for one the size and shape of Cinderella's carriage try 'Rouge Vif d'Etampes' and for even bigger, egg-shaped pumpkins grow 'Atlantic Giant' or 'Connecticut Field'. There are also white- and grey-skinned varieties for ghostly orbs. I let the children loose, cutting out ghoulish faces on their pumpkins, but my favourite method for a designer look is to use a core bit (used by plumbers to bore holes in walls for pipes) attached to an electric drill to create neat, Swiss cheese-style holes that let the candlelight spill out. If you haven't got a core bit, use an apple corer.

GROW YOUR OWN CHRISTMAS DINNER

If you grow your own vegetables, one of the best ways to welcome the festive season is with a home-grown Christmas feast. And if you don't grow your own vegetables then what better incentive do you need to start?

Many vegetables, such as leeks, parsnips and Brussels sprouts, are winter mainstays, but all it takes is a little advance planning to ensure you have an even wider variety to choose from come 25 December.

tip

If a white Christmas is forecast, dig up your root vegetables in advance and keep them in boxes of sand, protected from cats with mesh covers.

If Christmas was a colour then it would be red, so it seems right to include plenty of red or rich-purple vegetables on your plate. Here are some unusual festive vegetable varieties that are guaranteed to brighten up your Christmas feast:

- **Leek 'St Victor'.** An ornamental leek with frosted purple leaves.*
- **Brussels sprouts 'Falstaff'.** The buttons develop their purple-red colour after the first hard frost and keep it when they are cooked. They are also smaller than most other Brussels sprouts and have a mild, nutty flavour.*
- **Purple sprouting broccoli 'Extra Early Rudolph'.** This starts cropping from November and keeps growing right through to spring.*
- **Potato 'Cara'.** A lovely roasting potato with pink eyes. It can be harvested from August to September and stored in paper bags in a cool, frost-free place.
- **Ruby chard.** Lovely scarlet stems that are delicious steamed and tossed in butter.*
- **Onion 'Red Baron'.** The red baubles are picked in summer and stored in strings and will easily last until Christmas.
- **Red cabbage 'Rodeo F1'.** Delicious finely sliced and cooked in red wine with a splash of orange juice. Harvest it in November with the stem and keep it in water like a giant cut flower in a cool place.
- **Carrot 'Autumn King 2'.** This late maincrop variety might not be the reddest, but it is large and tasty. It can be left in the ground until Christmas, but if you don't want to take the risk of slugs and winter rot, lift and store them in boxes of sand. Don't forget to leave one out for the reindeer on Christmas Eve!
- **Swede 'Marian'.** A reliable and tasty winter crop that you can leave in the ground and pull on Christmas morning.*
- **Curly kale 'Redbor'.** This red-leaved kale is delicious steamed and smothered in butter. It is also brilliant for bringing Boxing Day bubble and squeak to life.*
- **Parsnip 'Gladiator'.** Parboiled, cored then roasted in lots of butter, Christmas wouldn't be the same without them.*

*denotes the vegetables that can be harvested on Christmas morning.
Follow the sowing guide on pp.154–55 for when to sow and pick these vegetables.

tip

Pick holly to adorn wreaths and decorate the house as soon as the berries redden to stop birds from getting them. Keep it like a bunch of flowers in a bucket of water in a shady spot outside and it will last for up to six weeks.

INDEX

ACKNOWLEDGMENTS

I'd like to thank the Ebury team – Lorna Russell, Caroline McArthur and Lara Maiklem – for their hard work crow-barring so much into these pages; Smith & Gilmour for a fantastic job on the design; 'good neighbours', Rich and Emma, Jan and brother Barry for their massive help; Dr Ian Bedford, for his advice and tests on killing pests; and, of course, the brilliant Jason Ingram, who is still washing the sand and salt from his tripod. Biggest thanks goes to Lisa who, as always, has been inspirational and a joy to work and live with.